WA 1253334 3

D1581748

Multimedia Computing

Crucial Study Texts for Computing Degree Courses

To order, please call our order line 0845 230 9000, or email orders@learningmatters.co.uk, or visit our website www.learningmatters.co.uk

Multimedia Computing

Daniel Cunliffe and Geoff Elliott

Computing series editor:
Peter Hodson

**Learning Resources
Centre**

1253334 3

First published in 2003 by Crucial, a division of Learning Matters Ltd.

All rights reserved. No part of this publication may be reproduced, stored in a retrieval system, or transmitted in any form or by any means, electronic, mechanical, photocopying, recording, or otherwise, without prior permission in writing from Learning Matters.

© Daniel Cunliffe and Geoff Elliott

British Library Cataloguing in Publication Data
A CIP record for this book is available from the British Library.

ISBN 1 903337 18 6

Cover design by Topics – The Creative Partnership
Project management by Deer Park Productions
Text design by Code 5 Design
Typeset by PDQ Typesetting, Newcastle under Lyme
Printed and bound by Bell & Bain Ltd, Glasgow

Learning Matters Ltd
33 Southernhay East
Exeter EX1 1NX
Tel: 01392 215560
Email: info@learningmatters.co.uk
www.learningmatters.co.uk

Contents

Chapter 1
Introduction

Chapter summary

Studying in higher education is hard work, but it should also be great fun – and multimedia provides more scope for fun than most subject areas within computing. In addition to using the latest hardware and software, you will also have the opportunity to be creative and imaginative.

In this chapter we give you an idea of what to expect in higher education and some ways of making your study as effective as possible. The emphasis is very much on you taking responsibility for your own learning and participating actively in your course. We look at what multimedia is and examine the overall process of multimedia authoring. We then consider some application areas, highlighting the interesting issues they raise for developers.

Learning outcomes

After studying this chapter you should aim to achieve these targets by answering the questions at the end of the chapter. You should be able to:

Outcome 1: Identify the characteristic features of multimedia applications.

Outcome 2: Recognise the potential for multimedia in different application areas and the challenges posed by those areas.

How will you be assessed on this?

In an exam you may be asked to define multimedia and describe its characteristic features. You may be asked to identify the different media types that may be used in a multimedia application.

In coursework you might be asked to develop an application, this should make good use of the characteristic features of multimedia. You would construct this application using an authoring tool and may be asked to describe how you have used that tool.

Section 1

Studying multimedia

Multimedia is a broad subject area containing a number of topics. Each course will place an emphasis on some topics and leave out others. It is important that you tailor your studies to suit the course you are on. You should be guided by your lecturer and the course syllabus. This syllabus will usually also include a schedule for the assessments and suggested reading.

━━━━━━━━━━━━━━ CRUCIAL TIP ━━━━━━━━━━━━━━

If you are given a syllabus keep hold of it. It can be useful for managing your time, planning your lecture preparation and guiding your revision.

Multimedia is a mixture of theoretical and practical knowledge and different courses will place a different balance on the theoretical and practical. This will be reflected in the way that you are taught, with lectures and seminars concentrating on the theoretical aspects and practical knowledge being learnt in lab-based sessions. It will also be reflected in the way you are assessed, with an exam assessing your knowledge of theory, whilst your practical skills are assessed through coursework.

Most courses will have a mixture of taught classes and self study time. Typically the time you have for self study is greater than the time you spend in taught classes. This time for self study is not free time, it is for you to work on assignments, revise for exams and do additional reading and research. Whilst you will receive guidance from your lecturers, you are responsible for deciding how you will use this time. One of the challenges you face is striking the right balance between time spent on study and time spent on other activities such as leisure and paid employment. When planning your time it is important to:

- **Prioritise and focus** – try to identify which are the most important or urgent things to do.

- **Schedule realistically** – recognise that there are times when you need to do other things and times when you need to relax.

- **Get started and get into a routine** – most people work well with a routine once they have settled into it.

- **Set achievable objectives** – break big tasks into small tasks, start with something small and easy, build up to more complex tasks.

- **Aim for quality not quantity** – time is not a good measure of effective study.

- **Reward yourself** – take time off or treat yourself as a reward for all your hard work.

One of the things you will need to do is balance the time you spend on exam revision against the time you spend on courseworks. Generally students do not spend enough time on revision and spend too much time making minor changes to courseworks which are not justified by the small increase in marks which is achieved. Revision should be an ongoing process throughout the course and should not be left to a short intensive period just before the exam.

━━━━━━━━━━━━━━ CRUCIAL TIP ━━━━━━━━━━━━━━

Your learning resources centre will have leaflets and books on study skills. They may also run study skills workshops.

In addition to developing your knowledge of theory and your practical knowledge, you will be expected to develop your intellectual abilities. This will be reflected in the things you are asked to do in exams and courseworks. At the beginning of your course you may be asked to 'describe' or 'state', as you progress you may be asked to 'explain', 'apply' or 'analyse' and finally to 'propose', 'evaluate', 'contrast' or 'critique'. Your assessment will move from testing your factual knowledge, through the application of that knowledge, to making judgements. You will often see these words used in assessments – look out for them as they tell you what you are expected to do.

Section 2

Learning from taught classes

The three most common types of taught class are the lecture, seminar and practical session.

- **A lecture** will be a large class during which the lecturer presents material to you verbally, typically supported by some visual aids. There will often be handouts associated with the lecture and time for questions at the end.

- **A seminar** is typically a smaller class than a lecture and generally takes the form of a discussion on a particular topic. Although the lecturer is likely to lead the seminar, you will be expected to take a more active part. This can take the form of answering questions, joining in the discussion, asking questions and presenting material. There may be handouts and there will often be reading that needs to be done beforehand.

- **Practical sessions** will generally be based in a computer lab or media production studio. During these sessions you will be using software or equipment. There may be worksheets for you to follow or demonstrations from the lecturer. Practical sessions are a good opportunity to ask the lecturer or your fellow students about any problems you are having.

There are some basic approaches that will help you to get the most from taught classes:

- **Prepare.** If the lecturer makes their notes available, get a copy and read through them. This will give you an idea of what to expect, you can identify any points that seem particularly complicated and you can prepare questions. It is particularly important to prepare for a seminar as there will often be something specific that you need to read. When reading for a seminar, it is useful to note down the key points and any questions. Sometimes the lecturer may give you questions to consider whilst reading; make notes of the key points that answer these questions.

- **Attend.** Some students make the mistake of thinking that everything they need is in the lecturer's notes – it isn't. The notes are intended to support the taught class, not replace it. The use of software and media equipment is central to your course, so attendance at practical classes is particularly important.

- **Make notes.** You cannot write down everything and you shouldn't try to. Instead you should be looking out for the key ideas, recurring themes and the relationships between different ideas. If your lecturer provides notes, it is useful to take these with you so that you can annotate them with your own explanations and examples, highlight the key ideas and so on. Sometimes there won't be notes and the lecturer will expect you to make your own notes.

- **Ask questions.** Asking questions is useful to clarify a point or to check your understanding. It can be quite intimidating to ask a question in front of a large class, but remember, if something isn't clear to you, it almost certainly isn't clear to other members your class either – you just happen to be the only person with enough courage to ask.

- **Organise and review.** It is worth checking through your notes fairly soon after the class to see if there is anything you need to add, highlight, or clarify. You should also file your notes and handouts carefully so that you can find material easily when you need it for revision or coursework.

Section 3

Books and the Web

Your lecturer will recommend books and Web sites, often on a topic by topic basis. Many multimedia books are expensive, so try to find out as much about a book as possible before deciding whether or not to buy it. You need to find a book that gives you the information you need, in the right format and at a price you can afford. Remember, your learning resources centre will contain many of the books you need.

When you are reading a book or Web site it is important to understand **why** you are reading it, because this will influence **how** you read it.

- **Set objectives** – try to define what information you are looking for and in what form.

- **Survey** – skim the material to get an overview of what it is about and how it is structured.

- **Focus** – select parts of the material that are relevant to your objectives and read these carefully.

- **Think and link** – how does the information relate to what you already know, does it raise new questions, does it meet your objectives? Make notes or add to your existing notes. Make sure you record the source of the information clearly so that you can return to it later if you need to.

There is a lot of useful material about multimedia, and using multimedia, on the Web. As well as being a useful source of information, Web sites can also be used as examples, case studies and inspiration for your own multimedia applications. There are some concerns over information on the Web. You need to be careful to check who wrote the material, whether it has a bias and how authoritative the information is.

When you use material created by someone else it is vital that you reference your source and do not use the material inappropriately. Your institution will have regulations regarding plagiarism (copying); make sure you understand them as the consequences of being caught for plagiarism can be severe.

Section 4

How to use this book

This book is aimed at helping you to study more effectively by focusing on the key concepts. All multimedia courses are different, because of this there may be some topics covered in this book which are not covered in your course. There may also be topics that you cover in your course that are only discussed briefly in this book. Assuming you have a course syllabus, one of the first things you should do is to map the chapters of this book to the topics covered in your course.

The remainder of this chapter looks at what multimedia is, how it is authored and application areas. The other chapters can be grouped into five main areas: hardware; the development process; the different media types, the Internet and World Wide Web; and advanced applications.

Hardware is discussed in Chapter 2, including the underlying technology, input and output devices and networks.

Different aspects of the **development process** are discussed in Chapters 3, 4, 5 and 6. Chapter 3 looks at the **development lifecycle**, what the actual process we follow is when developing a multimedia application. Chapter 4 looks at the **development team**, who the people involved in an application development are, what they do, and how the development process is managed. It also briefly considers **legal issues** and **budgeting**. Aspects of **multimedia design** are examined in Chapter 5, what needs to be designed, what goes into a good design. Chapter 6 looks at **development techniques**, the sort of design documents we produce, how these relate to multimedia design and development, how we use prototypes and how we evaluate our designs.

The different media types, **text**, **images**, **animation**, **audio** and **video** are covered in Chapters 7, 8, 9, 10 and 11 respectively. We examine why they might be used, technical issues in their creation and use, and the typical editing we will carry out.

Chapter 12 focuses on the **Internet** and the **World Wide Web**, providing an overview of the technology, specific application areas and HTML (the hypertext markup language).

Finally Chapter 13 looks at some **advanced applications** and **future developments**.

When you are studying a particular topic it is useful to read about it before the taught classes. You can use this book to give you an idea of what to expect and what the key concepts are. Some of the concepts may be hard to understand at first, but they will make more sense when they are discussed by your lecturer.

While you are studying a topic you can use this book to test your understanding of the key concepts and as a starting point for further reading and research that will deepen your understanding. Each chapter contains self-assessment questions with example answers.

Section 5

Defining multimedia

In this section we define the characteristic features of multimedia and how these features make multimedia different to other types of media. A well designed multimedia application combines these features effectively to create a powerful and sophisticated solution.

Multimedia is essentially about communication with people. In that sense it is nothing new, humans have been communicating for thousands of years using a range of techniques from cave paintings to text messaging. If we accept that it is just another form of communication, why is it that people are excited about multimedia?

CRUCIAL CONCEPTS

Multimedia applications communicate information to people using a **combination of different media**, often presented in a **non-linear form** and with **interactivity**. The rules and conventions of this **new medium** are not yet established.

Multimedia involves new combinations of media

As the name implies, multimedia is about the combination of different media types. Of course this is nothing new, this book is a mix of media types – it contains text, graphics and photographs. Multimedia is different in that it allows us to combine dynamic media (animation, sound, video) and static media (text, graphics, pictures) in a way that has not previously been possible.

When designing media combinations, we will typically be considering redundant media and complimentary media.

- **Redundant media** is where we use more than one medium to convey the same information. For instance we may have text on the screen, but also have an audio narration reading the text. This helps to reinforce the content and allows for different user preferences and abilities.

- **Complementary media** is where we use more than one medium and each conveys different information about the same topic. For instance we may have a photograph showing what an object looks like, text explaining what it is used for and an animation showing how it works. This allows us to use the medium most appropriate to the message.

	Static media	Dynamic media
Created electronically	Text Computer graphics	Synthesised audio Computer animation
Captured from the real world	Images	Natural audio Video

Figure 1.1 Different media types

Multimedia is a new medium

All media have conventions which have evolved over time. Things we take for granted, like page numbers and tables of contents, have had to be invented and become accepted. There are rules governing how these conventions are used by authors, and as readers we unconsciously make use of these rules – we know that the most important story in a newspaper is on the front page and will have the biggest headline (in the past newspapers didn't have headlines). In multimedia these conventions are still being established. This makes it interesting for developers (authors) as they can experiment to see what works. It makes it more difficult for users (readers) as they are not sure how to 'read' a multimedia application and there are often significant differences between applications.

Multimedia is non-linear communication

People often say that multimedia is non-linear and that this is what makes it different. A novel is a good example of a linear communication, the reader starts at the first page, continues through the fixed sequence of pages in order until they reach the end. If you alter the sequence, for example by reading the pages out of order, then they no longer make sense.

It is tempting to suggest that all books are linear communication because the pages are in a fixed order – but this is confusing the physical form (the way it has been put together) and the way it is used (how people read it). An obvious example of a book that is used in a non-linear way is an encyclopaedia. It would be very unusual to read an encyclopaedia from start to finish, instead we look up a term that we are interested in, read the 'chunk' of information about that term, possibly follow a cross reference to another term, and so on. The reader has opportunities to make choices about whether or not to follow a cross reference and, in moving about through the book, they are not following a linear sequence. Even when a book does provide a linear sequence, it may not be the only way of reading it. This book has a sequence, reading the chapters in order is one way in which you could read it. However you may well also use it in other, non-linear ways, you may use the index to look up a particular term, or you may use the table of contents to identify the chapter you want to read.

CRUCIAL TIP

Non-linearity refers to how something is used, rather than its physical form.

Multimedia applications will often provide methods for reading them in a non-linear way, but they don't have to. Sometimes we will want our user to read our content in a particular sequence. Within multimedia applications it is also possible to provide new methods for providing non-linear access, such as search facilities.

Multimedia is interactive

Multimedia is often interactive in that it involves the user doing something – they are not just viewing the application passively. Games are probably the most extreme example of interactive multimedia, but interactivity can be used for a variety of reasons, not just entertainment. Interactivity involves more than just clicking on the 'next page' button or selecting an option from a menu, it involves manipulating the content of the application. This aspect of multimedia isn't fully developed yet and the majority of multimedia applications are not truly interactive.

Quick test

1. What are the different dynamic and static media types?
2. What is the difference between linear and non-linear communication?

Section 6

Authoring multimedia

In this section we give an outline of the overall process of multimedia development in terms of creating digital media elements, authoring tools and their features, and basic choices for delivering our application to the user.

Multimedia applications are computer-based, both in their creation and in their use (though the machine we run the application on may not always look like a conventional computer). One implication of this is that we need to convert our analogue media, for example conventional video tape, into digital form so that they can be stored, edited and delivered in an application. The process of digitisation will require the use of specialist hardware, such as a video capture card, and software.

We will create some of our media directly in digital form, for example writing the text in a word processing package. This will require specialist software and sometimes specialist hardware, such as a graphics tablet.

One of the things we discover quite quickly is that digitised media elements can take up a lot of storage space. An approximate indication of the relative sizes of the different media types is shown in Figure 1.2. In fact we will often find that we need to make compromises between the media we would like to use and what is actually practical in terms of delivery to the user. The use of compression technologies is essential in multimedia.

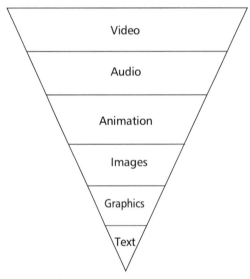

Figure 1.2 The approximate relative sizes of the media types

We will use a variety of specialist editing tools to manipulate our raw digital media into the desired form. We will then use multimedia authoring tools to assemble our media elements into an application which can be delivered to the user.

CRUCIAL CONCEPTS

Multimedia authoring involves the combination of **digitised media elements** to form a multimedia application. An application can be delivered over a **network** or stand-alone **on a local machine**.

There are a number of different authoring tools available and different tools give you a different perspective on how to build a multimedia application. The four main perspectives are:

- **Card-based** – individual cards (screens or pages) are created. Media elements are placed on the cards. Cards can be linked together to form paths that the user can follow. There are a number of screens, one or more of which will be displayed at one time.

- **Flowline-based** – individual screens and interface elements are represented as icons on a flowline which shows potential paths the user may follow. Media and interface elements are placed onto screens or directly onto the flowline. Again there are a number of different screens created.

- **Timeline-based** – media elements are arranged along a timeline which is then played like a movie. Effectively there is just a single screen which changes over time.

- **Object-based** – media elements are treated as individual objects which have properties and can be instructed to behave in certain ways. Again there is effectively just a single screen which changes over time.

Typical operations provided by an authoring tool include:

• arranging media elements on the screen	• providing transition effects between screens
• controlling appearance, behaviour, removal etc. of media elements	• changing the time dimension of dynamic media elements, making them faster or slower
• animating media elements	• programming or scripting to include more advanced behaviour
• importing different media types and file formats	• output in different formats, for example as a stand-alone executable, or for the web
• basic media creation, typically text and graphics	• synchronisation between different media elements
• basic editing for some media, for example controlling the volume of audio clips	• management facilities for the media elements in the application
• adding buttons, menus and other interface elements to the screen	• playing and providing an overview of application and the media elements

There are two basic delivery models for multimedia applications:

- **Networked** – the application runs on a server and users access it from remote machines via a network. Examples of this include Web sites and services available over mobile phones. Typical concerns with this form of delivery are the bandwidth of the network, the load on the server and lack of control over the delivery platform.

- **Local** – the application is placed on some form of physical storage medium (e.g. floppy disk, CD-ROM or DVD) and distributed to users, or is available to download via a network and install on a hard disk. Examples of this include computer games cartridges, educational software CD-ROMs and downloadable multimedia utilities. Typical concerns with this form of delivery are the capacity of the physical storage medium, the processing power of the local machine and the transfer rates from the storage medium.

Quick test

1. What are the relative sizes of the different media types?

2. What are the four main perspectives used in authoring tools?

3. What types of operation would a typical authoring tool provide?

Application areas

In this section we review some of the current application areas for multimedia and highlight the aspects that are of interest to multimedia developers.

─── CRUCIAL CONCEPTS ───

Multimedia is most appropriate where communication can be enhanced by one or more of: a **combination of media; non-linearity**; and **interactivity**. It also offers opportunities to **customise** the content or the application to suit the individual user. Different application areas provide different challenges to the developer.

Training and computer based learning

These applications are interested in finding combinations of media that communicate effectively and interactive activities that reinforce learning. We can create applications that allow trainees to experience situations that would be too expensive or too dangerous to conduct for real. Simulations can include media that makes the training more realistic, for example video, and decision-making under time pressures. There are also some interesting issues relating to customising content to suit the learner, based on their knowledge or performance in tests. In practice, interactivity is only used in fairly limited ways.

E-commerce

E-commerce can bring benefits for customers as well as retailers, particularly where information is customised to suit an individual customer. Allowing customers to express their personal preferences enables the retailer to target them with products that they are more likely to be interested in. We can use different media to preview and demonstrate the product. We can allow the customer to buy online. On the Web we need to make people want to visit our site, and importantly to revisit it.

Public access applications

Information kiosks are becoming increasingly popular in museums, libraries, train stations, trade shows and, in some cases, on the street. We need to attract the user's attention, often in a noisy or busy environment. The application needs to be very usable, there is no opportunity to provide training, the user is unlikely to want to use a help system, they just want to be able to walk up to it and use it. We may need to cater for a wide variety of different users, of different ages and abilities, looking for different kinds of information. The user is unlikely to spend very long using the application, we need to get our information across quickly and clearly.

Games

Sometimes games are not seen as serious multimedia applications, but in many ways they are some of the most advanced. Interactivity is a key feature of games and typically the interactivity in a game is complex and sophisticated. We need to engage the user (get their interest and keep it). This is achieved partly through the interactivity and game play, but also through the creation of a strong visual identity and good use of audio. Although games tend to make relatively little use of text and images, they generally make good use of graphics, animation, audio and sometimes video. They provide good examples of how the different media types can be used together effectively.

Section 8

End of chapter assessment

Multiple choice questions

1. Dynamic media –

    a) are created electronically
    b) are played over time
    c) are captured from the real world
    d) change every time they are viewed.

2. Computer graphics are –

    a) static media, created electronically
    b) dynamic media, created electronically
    c) static media, captured from the real world
    d) dynamic media, captured from the real world.

3. A truly interactive multimedia application is one which –

    a) allows the user to play a game
    b) includes mostly dynamic media
    c) allows the user to manipulate the content
    d) uses menus to help the user move about.

4. Non-linear communication –

    a) takes the reader through the content in a fixed order
    b) takes the user through the content in a random order
    c) allows the user to choose the order in which they read content
    d) uses menus to help the user move through the content.

Multiple choice answers

1. b) is the right answer. Dynamic media may be captured from the real world or created electronically, but so are static media.

2. a) is the right answer (see Figure 1.1).

3. c) is the right answer. The others may be true for particular interactive applications, but they need not be in general.

4. c) is the right answer. d) may be true for a particular application, but it need not be in general.

Questions

1. Define multimedia and compare it with other forms of media.

2. A large corporation is considering employing your multimedia development company to produce a staff training application on fire safety and fire fighting. Briefly describe the ways in which you would use multimedia for such an application and identify the potential benefits of using multimedia.

Answers

1. We are being asked to *define the characteristic features of multimedia* and to *compare it with other media forms*. We can use the subsection headings in Section 5 of this chapter to guide us:

    • multimedia involves new combinations of media (dynamic and static);
    • multimedia is a new medium;
    • multimedia is non-linear communication (use not physical form);
    • multimedia is (or should be) interactive.

When we are describing these features, we need to remember to compare them with other media forms, such as books, cinema and television. We don't need to compare multimedia to every alternative form of media, just those that make an interesting comparison. Referring back to Section 5, we can see that many of the features of multimedia can also be found in other media types, this should also be in our answer.

2. The two things this question is asking us to do are *describe the ways we would use multimedia* and *identify potential benefits*. We also need to consider the scenario that we have been given – a large corporation will have a large number of employees so training them in traditional ways will be expensive. Fire safety and fire fighting may involve dangerous situations that are hard to simulate in traditional training approaches. We are also likely to want to test that a member of staff has understood the training.

In describing the ways we would use multimedia, we need to consider the different media types and the characteristic features of multimedia, particularly non-linear communication and interactivity.

Ways we might use different media types include:

- using text to convey key information;
- using graphics and images to show hazardous situations and fire fighting equipment;
- using computer animation to demonstrate how fires spread and how fire fighting equipment is operated;
- using video to show equipment in use.

We can include non-linear communication and interactivity in several ways, including:

- A timed test where the user is presented with a short video clip after which they need to make a choice of which action to take, which is then followed by another video clip showing the consequences of their action.
- A series of test questions with multiple choice answers. Depending on the answer the user gives, we may make them revise material again.
- A simulation of an office environment in which the user can experiment to see the effects of leaving fire doors open, fires starting in different places, and so on.

Potential benefits include:

- cost savings for the corporation;
- standardisation of training;
- training that can be conducted at a time convenient for staff;
- assessment of staff understanding;
- the ability to test staff in dangerous situations without exposing them to harm.

Even though the question does not specifically ask us to, we can also mention any disadvantages of using multimedia. One obvious disadvantage is that a video of a fire is far less frightening than the real thing. We may want to use our multimedia training package alongside traditional training methods rather than as a replacement.

When answering this type of question you can be a bit imaginative. As you are not actually being asked to build the application you can include features that you don't know how to create, so long as they are not too fanciful.

Section 9

Further reading and research

Reading

Bucknall, K. (1996) *Studying at University*, How To Books Ltd.
Race, P. (1996) *500 Tips for Students*, Blackwell Publishers.
Race, P. (1999) *How to get a Good Degree*, Open University Press.

Research

Visit your learning resources centre, ask about study skills guides and courses. Also ask about the availability of old exam papers. Familiarise yourself with the location of the multimedia books and journals. Remember the books needed for multimedia are likely to be in a number of different locations.

Maintain a portfolio of your multimedia work. This should include electronic copies of media elements and applications that you create and examples of the design documents you produce. A portfolio is useful for showing to potential employers, you could even create a CD-ROM version to send with your CV.

Chapter 2
Multimedia hardware

Chapter summary

This chapter provides an overview of the hardware required for multimedia development and delivery. Studying this chapter will help you to understand all the various issues related to multimedia hardware and be able to compare the differences between hardware for multimedia development and delivery.

Learning outcomes

After studying this chapter you should aim to achieve these targets by answering the questions at the end of the chapter. You should be able to:

Outcome 1: Compare and contrast different types of computer used for multimedia development.

Outcome 2: Describe the main input and output devices used in multimedia development and delivery.

Outcome 3: Outline the role of networks in multimedia development and delivery.

Outcome 4: Summarise the main end user hardware issues.

How will you be assessed on this?

In an exam you might have to suggest what hardware would be appropriate for multimedia development and be able to roughly describe the specification of a suitable computer system for a given scenario. In course work you might have to explain what hardware you used to complete a project or explain for what end user hardware you have designed your application.

Section 1

Computers

In this section you will learn about the specification of computers and their use in multimedia development and delivery.

The two types of **desktop computer** used for multimedia development are the **Apple Mac** and the Microsoft Windows based **personal computer** or **PC.** Both platforms share these common components as do most types of computer:

• **Processor**	The processor or central processing unit is the key component and controls the rest of the computer and executes programs.
• **Cache**	Cache is a small amount of very high speed memory built into the processor for doing immediate calculations.
• **RAM memory**	RAM (random access memory) is the working memory where the current application program resides.
• **System bus**	The system bus connects all the necessary devices to the processor. There are other buses that connect to the system bus like SCSI for hard drives.
• **Motherboard**	The processor, cache, RAM and system bus all reside on a main printed circuit board called the motherboard.
• **Operating system**	The operating system manages the loading and unloading of applications and files and the communication with other peripheral devices like printers.
• **Storage devices**	Application programs and working files are saved longer term on different kinds of storage device. Storage devices include hard disk drives, CD-ROMs and floppy drives.
• **Input/output devices**	Connected to the system bus are a number of other devices that control the other essential components of a desk top computer including the monitor, mouse, keyboard, speakers, printer, scanner.
• **Expansion bus**	Most desktops should include 'slots' into which other non-standard devices can be installed.

The latest specification Macs and PCs are capable of running the application tools necessary for developing standard multimedia applications. The standard applications are image, sound and video editing, animation and multimedia integration. Comparisons of the performance of the latest generation of PCs and Macs are hotly contested but in general they are now roughly the same with each type of computer performing better on some tasks than others. Apple Macs have, in the past, been more associated with the multimedia industry, however PCs are increasingly being used since they are now capable of undertaking the same processor intensive tasks like video compression equally well. High specification computers are required to undertake some of the tasks required in multimedia development and Figure 2.1 shows the specification of a recent PC and Mac base unit that are appropriate.

PC	Mac
Based on an Intel Pentium P3 processor running at a clockspeed of 1GHz or the AMD Athlon at 1.4GHz	Based on two Motorola PowerPC G4 processors running at clockspeed of 1 Ghz
128Kbyte L1 and 256Kbyte L2 cache	32Kbyte L1 Kbyte L2 and 2Mbyte L3 cache
512Mbyte Ram expandable to 2Gbyte	512Mbyte Ram expandable to 2Gbyte
System bus is the peripheral components interface or PCI	System bus is the peripheral components interface or PCI
Microsoft Windows XP operating system	Apple MacOS X operating system
Storage devices: 1. 60Gbyte hard drive connected via a SCSI or Ultra ATA/100 interface. 2. CD-ROM writer	Storage devices: 1. 60Gbyte hard drive connected via an Ultra ATA/100 interface 2. CD-ROM writer
4 PCI expansion slots	4 PCI expansion slots

Figure 2.1 Specification of the base unit of recent PCs and Macs suitable for multimedia development

There are other types of computer used in multimedia developed particularly for graphics processing, video capture, and editing and 3D modelling. For example, the **SGI Silicon Graphics Octane2** computer is specifically designed for visualisation, 3D modelling and other graphical applications and is based on SGI's own R14000A processor and a version of the UNIX operating system. 300 SGI Octane2 computers were used to create the 3D animated characters for Disney and Pixar's *Toy Story 2* film.

There are a number of storage devices used in multimedia development, the key one being the **hard disk drive**. It is important to have a large hard disk drive to undertake some tasks like video and sound editing, however the latest desktop computers come with a minimum of 60Gbyte of capacity which is enough for most standard tasks. Currently, hard disk drives have capacities up to 120Gbytes and data transfer rates of 160Mbits per second. There two standard types of hard drive used in desktop computers – enhanced integrated drive electronics (EIDE) or Ultra ATA based drives and small computer system interface (SCSI) based drives.

Optical disk drives including the **compact disk-ROM (CD-ROM)**, **CD-Recordable (CR-R)**, **CD-Rewriteable (CD-RW)** and the **digital versatile disk drives (DVD)** are also key storage devices. The CD-ROM was the standard medium for delivering multimedia throughout much of the 1990s but is being superseded by the rapid development of the Web. Computers used for multimedia development should include a CD-RW drive for reading and writing CD-ROMs disks. CD-R drives, sometimes called WORM (write once read many) drives, are used for backup purposes and also for creating master copies of multimedia applications. For batch production purposes CD-Copiers are used for copying and labelling 50 CDs at once. CD-ROM drives store up to 660Mbyte at access speeds of up to 7200Kbits per second. Currently CD-RW drives work at lower access speeds but are becoming standard since they are re-recordable and are making the 3.5'' floppy drive redundant. CDs are all based on a particular **CD standard** named after the colour of its covers. The original audio CD was based on the yellow book standard, the CD-ROM on the red book but is also compatible with the yellow book standard so you can listen to audio CDs on your computer. CD-R and CD-RW are based on the orange book standard. It is likely that DVD drives and in particular DVD rewriteable drives will eventually supersede CD-ROM technology with storage capacities up to 17Gbyte and faster transfer speeds.

─── CRUCIAL CONCEPTS ───

Desktop computer: a computer that sits on desktops and that contains a processor, RAM, system bus, motherboard, operating system, storage devices and input and output devices. Multimedia desktop computers must be of a high specification. **CD standards** are the yellow, red and orange books which specify the audio, CD-ROM and CD-RW formats for optical disk technology.

─── CRUCIAL TIP ───

Search the Web sites of computer manufacturers like Apple and Dell and find out what are the latest specifications of desktop computers. Then search the Web to find out about what the specifications listed mean, e.g. what is a RAID drive?

Quick test

What are the main storage devices used in multimedia development?

Section 2

Input devices

The last section discussed the key specifications of computers used in multimedia development. In this section we consider the various input devices which are attached to a computer for multimedia development and delivery.

Keyboards

Input devices enable users to input different kinds of data from text through to video into a computer. **Keyboards** have not changed in layout since the QWERTY arrangement of the nineteenth century although there have been several attempts at improving its layout. The design of the keyboards has improved with cordless and ergonomically contoured keyboards like that shown in Figure 2.2.

Figure 2.2 Ergonomically contoured keyboard

Pointing devices

There are a range of **pointing devices** used in multimedia development and delivery. The classic pointing device is the mouse which is now available cordless and is based on an optical sensor rather than a rolling ball. Multimedia developers who are engaged in image or video editing may wish to use more sophisticated pointing devices like a trackerball or tablet. Figure 2.3 shows a state of the art trackerball which gives developers finer control over the position of the pointer without moving their hands.

Figure 2.3 State of the art trackerball

The other pointing device used by developers is the **digitising tablet** as shown in Figure 2.4. Either a special pen or a mouse is used as the pointing device allowing developers to map the dimensions of the tablet to the dimensions of the screen so that extreme points of the tablet match the extreme points of the screen. Multimedia developers can place pictures onto the digitising tablet and 'trace' them if they need to.

Figure 2.4 Digitising tablet with mouse and pen

Sound recording equipment

The use of sound in its various forms is a component of a multimedia application and the quality of the recording equipment is important in determining the final quality of the sound. **Sound recording equipment** ranges from a simple tape cassette recorder for low budget amateur sound productions to a fully equipped professional recording studio. The essential pieces of hardware for recording sound are microphones or musical instruments for creating the sound source, portable recording equipment like a digital audio tape (DAT) recorder for use outside a studio, a multitrack **mixing console** for editing and mixing various sources of sound and another storage device like a DAT recorder. **DAT recorders** enable sound to be recorded at sampling rates up to 96KHz and 16 bits per sample. The medium for the recording, editing and capture of music is generally undertaken using the MIDI data format and today most electronic instruments and equipment associated with music support it. Chapter 10 explains how MIDI works.

Once the sound has been recorded it must be input into a computer for further editing and integration into a multimedia application. Output from digital sources like a DAT recorder can be input directly into a computer without conversion, however analogue sources need to be captured, i.e. converted from analogue to digital. Standard **sound cards** installed in most desktop computers can receive and convert analogue sound sources. Sound cards have a number of different input sockets for various sound sources and can support sample frequencies up to 192KHz at 24 bits per sample. Sound cards also convert sound from digital to analogue for output to speakers.

Video recording equipment

The hardware used in professional video production is beyond the scope of this book so we focus on the kind of equipment that could be used by a small independent multimedia design company or home users. Basic **video recording equipment** includes either an analogue or **digital video camera** and a **video capture card** installed in a desktop computer. Video capture cards are different to graphic display cards which are not capable of video capture. Although many video experts still prefer using analogue cameras, digital video cameras are becoming more standard offering 6Mb/s data rate or up to 30 frames per second at a resolution of 720 by 480 pixels. Once a piece of video has been recorded it needs to be captured; digital video cameras can be connected directly to one of the USB or serial ports on the desktop computer but analogue video needs to be captured via a video capture card. Video capture cards receive analogue video signals through one of their ports and sample it at a frequency up to 30 frames per second, a resolution of 768 by 576 pixels and a sample size of 24 bits per pixel. Video capture requires high specification desktop computers with a fast, high capacity hard disk drive to cope with the input video data.

Image scanners

The last type of input device used in multimedia development which you should be aware of are **image scanners**. Scanners enable developers to digitise hard copies of pictures and photographs ready for editing and inclusion in multimedia projects. Standard flatbed scanners (see Figure 2.5) are available in up to A3 size and scan up to 2400 dots per inch (dpi) with a colour depth of up to 48 bits per pixel.

Figure 2.5 UMAX Astra 4700 Flatbed Scanner

CRUCIAL CONCEPTS

Pointing device: a range of devices used with PCs and Macs that include mouse, trackerballs and digitising tablets.

Sound recording equipment includes sound recorders like DAT or tape cassette, various microphones, mixing consoles that are used to create sound for multimedia applications.

Video recording equipment includes the various hardware used to create digital video, including analogue and digital video cameras, analogue and digital editing studios, video cassette players and video capture cards.

CRUCIAL TIP

Visit www.pctechguide.com to learn about input devices in detail.

Quick test

What kind of pointing devices do multimedia developers use and why?

Section 3

Output devices

In this section we consider the various output devices which are attached to a computer for multimedia development and delivery.

Monitors

The most important output device for multimedia development and delivery is the **monitor**. Thus the quality of monitors and the **graphic display cards** that drive them are important considerations for multimedia developers. Multimedia developers need to use large 17'' or 19'' (measured diagonally across the screen) monitors in order to have room to display the multimedia application under development and the various dialogue boxes of the authoring tools. Some multimedia developers use two monitors that are driven using special graphics cards so that they can see the multimedia application on one screen and have the tools displayed on the other.

Large monitors do not necessarily mean that more information can be displayed. The amount of detail displayed on a monitor is dictated by its screen resolution and the resolution that the graphics display card is capable of delivering. See Chapter 8 for an explanation of the meaning of resolution. Multimedia development needs large monitors that support high screen resolutions and a large number of colours. Currently, the most common standard for graphic display cards on PCs used for multimedia development is the **Ultra Extended Graphics Array** or UXGA which enables a monitor to display 1600 by 1200 pixels and up to 16.7 million colours. There are a number of other competing standards. Graphic display cards have their own special RAM which contains the current screen display pixel by pixel. Some multimedia tasks, like video and image editing and displaying 3D graphics, require between 4 and 8Mbytes of graphic display RAM.

An important type of monitor for use in point of information applications are **touch screens** which are both input and output devices. Touch screens are an intuitive way for users to interact with a multimedia application by allowing them to touch buttons and links directly rather than indirectly via a mouse or other pointing device. Touch screens include three key components:

- a touch screen sensor panel that generates a voltage to indicate where the screen was touched;
- a controller that converts the voltage into a digital signal and transmits it to the processor; and
- a software driver to translate the digital signal into data that emulates the mouse.

There is one other type of monitor which is used in public multimedia presentations called a **data projector.** Data projectors enable the normal output from a computer to be projected onto a large screen so that a larger audience can see. Some data projectors include special display screens which act like enormous digitising tablets so the display can be used as if it were a touch screen.

Speakers

Another crucial output device for multimedia applications are the **speakers** which provide the sound outputs. Speakers are driven by sound cards as explained in the last section. Most sound cards support the **SoundBlaster** standard developed by Creative Labs and the General MIDI standard (see Chapter 10 for an explanation of MIDI) for sound reproduction. Speakers used with desktop computers usually require their own power source and have built-in amplifiers.

Printers

The last type of output device used in multimedia is the **printer**. For multimedia development it is important to have a high quality colour printer to show screen shots to clients and for discussing particular elements of a multimedia project. It is impossible for a printer to exactly match the on-screen colours, however they are helpful in seeing the general look and feel of an application. There are two types of colour printer - laser and inkjet. Currently a top of the range inkjet printer is capable of outputing about 1.5 pages per minute at a quality of 1200 by 600 dpi and a similar priced colour laser can output four pages per minute at a quality of 600 by 600 dpi. The new inkjet and colour laser printers allow you to change each of the colour cartridges (cyan, magenta, yellow and black) separately. The latest inkjet printers also allow you to purchase each of the colour print heads and associated ink cartridges separately hence reducing the cost of printing. Currently colour laser printers have a lower cost per page than an equivalent inkjet printer.

CRUCIAL CONCEPT

Graphics display cards are installed in desktop computers and drive the monitor. The most up to date standard is the ultra extended graphics array.

Quick test

What kinds of monitors are used for multimedia development?

Section 4

Networks

In most multimedia design studios computers and peripheral devices are generally networked together. Therefore you should have some understanding of the principles of local area networks. Also the Web has become an important medium for delivering multimedia so you should have some understanding of the hardware used in the Web and the Internet.

Computers and other devices in multimedia design studios are often networked together to enable people to share files and devices. A **network** simply means that a group of computers and other devices like printers are linked together, usually by cable which allows people to send files of data to each other and to share devices. A network that only extends to a room or single building is referred to as a **local area network** or **LAN**. Typically, each computer in a network has a **network interface card** (NIC) installed in one of their expansion slots to which a network cable is attached. The most common type of network is based on the Ethernet protocol which defines the rules by which each computer can use the network to avoid more than one computer trying to use the network simultaneously. Figure 2.6 shows a typical network used in a multimedia design studio and includes a file server, scanner and several printers. A **file server** is a special computer with a large storage capacity where designers usually save their work rather than on their local computer so that they can be available to everyone else in the studio. The hard disk drives of file servers need to be fast so they tend use a different type of bus like SCSI or RAID. Often one or two of the computers in a design studio serve a dedicated purpose so for example, one of the computers in Figure 2.6 is a dedicated video editing suite which can be used when needed and enabling any files produced to be placed on the file server.

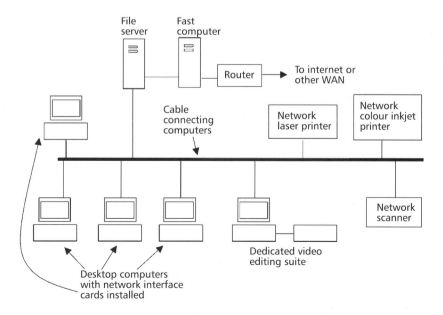

Figure 2.6 A multimedia design studio network

A network which extends over a broader geographic area is referred to as **wide area network** (WAN), a good example being the Internet. Chapter 12 explains what hardware is .involved in the Internet and the Web. To enable designers to connect to a WAN, particularly the Internet, a **router** is included in the LAN configuration as shown in Figure 2.6. A router is usually a fast computer with at least one network interface card and at least one WAN interface card.

CRUCIAL CONCEPTS

Network: An arrangement of computers and other devices linked together via a cable enabling files and devices to be shared.
Local area network (LAN): A network limited to one room or building.
Wide area network (WAN): a network which extends over a large geographic area.

Quick test

What are the benefits of a local area network in a multimedia design studio?

CRUCIAL TIP

Practise drawing the diagram of a network in Figure 2.6.

Section 5

End user hardware issues

So far we have focused on hardware designed for multimedia development. However there are a number of important end user hardware considerations of which a multimedia designer should be aware.

Multimedia designers will be using high specification computers with large, high quality monitors. However the end users' hardware will most probably be of lower specification and use different input and output devices. It is therefore important that designers define the **minimum specification** they are designing for. Ideally a minimum specification computer is set up somewhere in the design studio to check the performance of an application. Figure 2.7 gives a breakdown of the **end user hardware issues** of the various elements of hardware.

So far, we have been assuming the end user will have a desktop computer. However many multimedia applications are often placed in public spaces like museums, libraries or airports. A multimedia application that is found in a public space is referred to as a **multimedia kiosk** or **point of information terminal** (POI). The important hardware issue to consider when designing a multimedia kiosk is the higher levels of usage and therefore the need for more durable hardware. Generally kiosks are enclosed in a cabinet so end users cannot interfere with the computer. However the output devices (monitor, speakers) and the input devices (pointing devices) could be. So the monitors, keyboards, speakers and pointing devices must be robust to cope with heavy usage. Since mice require some maintenance touch screens (see Section 2) are often used as the pointing device. If the application requires the end user to carry out drag and drop actions a trackerball might be embedded in the kiosk cabinet. Purpose built keyboards are sometimes used with a limited number of keys to provide for the actions used in the application like navigation buttons.

Element	Issues
• **Processor**	The developers' computers will be using high specification processors. The end users' computers will use processors from different manufacturers running at different speeds. Developers should therefore be careful not to optimise their applications for a particular processor or chipset.
• **RAM memory**	Developers must make sure their applications do not require an unreasonable amount of RAM to run efficiently.
• **Operating system**	Differences in operating system are very problematic for developers and could mean producing more than one version of an application.
• **Storage devices**	Recent hard disk drives of at least 10Gb are generally of sufficient capacity to cope with typical multimedia applications. However many end users will have relatively low speed CD-ROM drives so developers must make sure that their applications will run adequately on low specification CD-ROM drives or arrange for the install program to copy files which require fast access on to the end users' hard disk drives.
• **Monitor**	This is one of the most important considerations for designers. Designers will be working with large 19″ or dual monitors at high screen resolutions supporting 24 bit colour. A significant proportion of end users will have a 15″ monitors, running at lower screen resolution and maybe only 8 bit colour depth. It is imperative designers test out their materials with a low specification monitor and declare a minimum standard for end users.
• **Pointing devices**	As noted developers tend to use digitising tablets or trackerballs for extra precision. End users will in general be using mice. Applications should be tested out using mice.

Figure 2.7 End user hardware issues

--- CRUCIAL CONCEPTS ---

Minimum specification is a list of the hardware requirements that a particular application needs to run properly.

End user delivery issues are the list of issues designers must consider when designing their applications, perhaps the key one is the resolution and colour depth of the monitor.

Multimedia kiosk/point of information terminal are multimedia applications placed in public spaces. The hardware used must be robust to withstand heavy usage.

Quick test

What should multimedia designers be aware of when designing for end users?

Section 6

End of chapter assessment

Multiple choice questions

1. Which of the following is true about desktop computers?

    a) The SGI Octane2 is the most commonly used multimedia computer.

    b) 32Mb of RAM is sufficient for most multimedia development work.

    c) Multimedia development computers should include an expansion bus.

    d) Multimedia development computers do not need an operating system.

2. Which of the following statements is true about storage devices?
   a) Hard disk drive capacity should be at least 60Gb for multimedia development.
   b) There are two standard types of hard disk drive – PCI and SCSI.
   c) CD-Rs are based on the yellow book standard.
   d) CD-ROM technology is superior to DVD technology.

3. Which of the following statements is true about input devices used for multimedia development?
   a) Image scanners are used for displaying images.
   b) Graphic display cards are capable of video capture.
   c) Sound cards are capable of sound capture and output.
   d) Multimedia designers only use mice as pointing devices.

4. Which of the following statements is true of display devices used in multimedia development?
   a) Developers generally use touch screens.
   b) The screen resolution dictates the number of displayable colours.
   c) Graphic display cards have their own RAM.
   d) Large monitors are required to displayed more information.

5. Which of the following is true about a networked multimedia studio?
   a) Each computer needs a network interface card.
   b) Each computer needs a file server.
   c) The Internet is an example of a LAN.
   d) Generally each computer on a network has its own printer and scanner.

6. Which of the following statements is true of end user's hardware:
   a) The end user's specification will not be the same as the designer's.
   b) Designers should decide on a minimum specification.
   c) Most end users have 19'' monitors.
   d) Multimedia kiosks use standard desktop input and output devices.

Multiple choice answers

1. c)
2. a)
3. c)
4. c)
5. a)
6. b)

Exercises

1. You have been asked to come up with the specification of a new design studio for a large company who want to produce multimedia training applications for their staff. Write down and explain your choices of hardware.

2. You are designing an interactive multimedia application that will be made available over the Web. Write down the kinds of issues you need to consider about the end users' hardware.

3. What extra hardware or equipment is required to produce digital sound and video?

Answers

1. This question gives you a lot of scope to explain what you know about the hardware required to undertake development work. You could start by considering whether to choose Apple or PC based computers and their respective specifications. Once you have considered this you can write down the choices of input and output devices, especially sound and video recording and editing equipment. A set-up like this would require a network so you should reproduce and explain a diagram similar to that in Figure 2.6. If this design studio is producing training materials for its staff it will need to make its materials available. This will either by via the Web, in which case they will need a HTTP server, on the network (see Chapter 12) or a multiple CD copier.

2. You should start your answer by explaining the issues of bandwidth (see Chapter 12) and the problems of knowing what are the end users' computer configurations. If the application is going to be interactive, the end user must have computer hardware that can cope with the (i) the time to download interactive applications (ii) running the application. You should suggest the need to stipulate a minimum specification for running the application. Now you can consider what that minimum specification should be so you can discuss the screen resolution, processor, amount of RAM, hard disk drive and variations in operating system and browser.

3. To answer this question fully it is helpful to have read and understood Chapters 10 and 11 on sound and video. To produce digital sound you need to consider the equipment used to record the required sound – e.g. DAT recorder, sound studio setup and the issue of MIDI or digital audio; the equipment used to edit the sound either digital or analogue including a mixing desk; and the hardware required to capture the sound track – sound card, reproduction equipment to connect up to the sound card and a desktop computer capable of capturing and storing sound. A better answer would include a brief overview of the process of editing digital sound found in Chapter 10. The situation for digital video is similar. Explain what equipment is used to record video and capture video. Video capture is one of the most demanding tasks for a desktop computer so you should explain that a high specification computer is required and suggest a suitable specification. Unlike sound capture, where the sound card can both output and receive sound, video capture generally requires a dedicated card separate to the display card which has a significant amount of on board memory.

Section 7

Further reading

Buchanan, W. (1999) *Mastering Networks*, Macmillan.
Englander, I. (2000) *Architecture of Computer Hardware and Systems Software: An IT Approach (2nd edition)*, John Wiley and Sons.

Chapter 3
Multimedia
development lifecycle

Chapter summary

In this chapter we look at the multimedia development process. First we look at some of the factors that make multimedia developments challenging. We then outline the stages of a typical development, emphasising the iterative nature of the development process.

Learning outcomes

After studying this chapter you should aim to achieve these targets by answering the questions at the end of the chapter. You should be able to:

> **Outcome 1: Recognise the characteristics of multimedia development.**
>
> **Outcome 2: Describe and apply the stages of a typical multimedia development lifecycle.**

How will you be assessed on this?

In an exam you may be asked to explain why multimedia development is different to other types of project development, or what particular challenges face the project manager. You may be asked to outline the overall lifecycle and discuss the issues faced by developers at each stage.

In coursework that required you to build a multimedia application, you might be expected to show that your development process has fully considered the distinctive characteristics of multimedia development. You are also likely to develop a better application if you follow an appropriate development process.

Section 1

Multimedia application development

In this section we examine some of the characteristics of the multimedia development process that make it more challenging to manage than other types of project. If we are aware of these characteristics, we can ensure that the final product meets the needs of its users and our clients, is of sufficiently high quality, is delivered on time and within budget.

--- CRUCIAL CONCEPTS ---

Multimedia development is complex and requires **good communication** between the **technical** and **creative** members of the **development team** and with both **clients** and **users**. The success of a development can be measured in terms of **quality**, time of **delivery** and **cost**.

Multimedia development is complex because multimedia applications are complex. Multimedia itself is still an emerging concept; we are still exploring what is possible, what works and what doesn't work. The technology we are working with is constantly changing, providing new challenges for the technical team and new opportunities for the creative team. Multimedia involves the combination of the creative and the technical, two areas that typically have very different ways of working and different ways of communicating ideas. Each area may lack an understanding of the difficulties and limitations faced by the other. Good project management and teamwork are essential in multimedia development.

A multimedia development involves three important sets of people: the **multimedia development company**; the **clients** who are paying the development company to develop the application; and the **user** or **customer** who will be using or buying the application.

The success of the development process can be measured along three axes:

- **Quality** – are the client and the users satisfied with the final application?
- **Delivery** – was the application delivered on time with respect to the contract agreed with the clients?
- **Cost** – was the application delivered within the budget agreed with the client and allowing the development company to make a profit?

These three axes form the cost-delivery-quality cube (Figure 3.1). Any particular development can be placed within this cube.

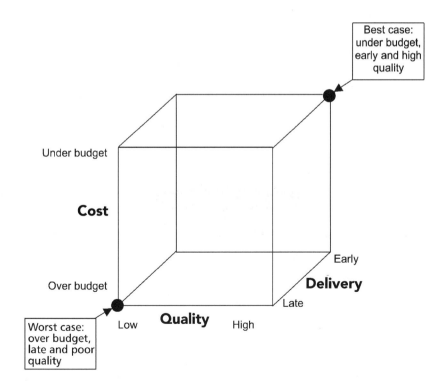

Figure 3.1 The cost-delivery-quality cube

The key factor in achieving a successful process is **communication**, both within the development team and with the clients and users (Figure 3.2).

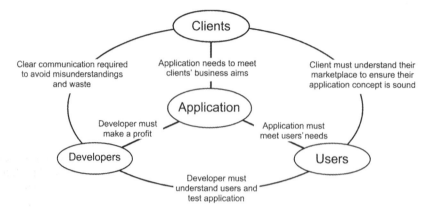

Figure 3.2 Communication between clients, users and developers

The development process includes regular opportunities for the developers to communicate with both clients and users. The development process is also iterative, meaning that we may need to design, test and redesign and retest many times within the development. Since we do not know beforehand how many times this will be necessary, it is difficult to plan and budget for and may put pressure on deadlines. It may also be hard to explain the need for this to the clients who wishes the development to be completed quickly and cheaply.

Every multimedia development is unique, so every development process is unique, making it hard to adopt a standard process and to learn lessons from one development that can be applied to subsequent developments.

Quick test

1. Who are the three important sets of people involved in a multimedia application development?

2. What are the three axes along which the success of a development process can be measured?

Development lifecycle

In this section we will describe a typical multimedia development lifecycle. Communication with clients and users will be an important part of this process.

--- CRUCIAL CONCEPTS ---

The **development lifecycle** can be broken down into four main stages: **bidding; development; launch; and maintenance**. An **iterative cycle** of **designing, evaluating, re-designing** and **re-evaluating** during the development phase is central to ensuring that users can use the application and will want to.

The development lifecycle can be broken down into different stages. The boundaries between the stages are somewhat arbitrary and different development teams may adopt slightly different stages, or call them by different names, but the actual work that is done will be broadly the same. We have chosen to consider the lifecycle as four main stages (Figure 3.3).

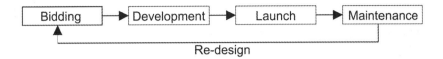

Figure 3.3 Lifecycle stages

The **bidding** stage covers the period from the initial client approach, to the acceptance of our proposal and the signing of contracts. Most of the communication in this stage is between the developers and the clients. The **development** stage is where we design, implement and evaluate our ideas for the application, resulting in a complete application. Most of the communication in this stage is between the developers and the users, though there will also be significant communication between the developers and the clients. The **launch** stage includes the release of the application. The final stage is **maintenance** which is concerned with the application once it has been launched, updating content, fixing any problems which weren't detected earlier, evolving the application to suit new client and user needs. This will involve communication between the developers and both users and clients, and between the users and clients.

Bidding

The bidding stage starts with the initial client contact. This may be a direct contact from the client, or indirectly through publication of an invitation to tender for the contract. The bidding process may often be a competitive process with more than one development company bidding for the contract. In other cases the developers may be the only company approached by client.

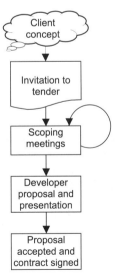

Figure 3.4 Bidding stage

The project manager needs to prepare a proposal that meets the clients' brief, has an achievable deadline and sufficient budget. It is therefore essential that the clients' requirements and expectations are fully understood. This is achieved through a series of **scoping meetings** between the project manager and the business manager and the clients. Members of the technical and creative teams and legal advisors may also be involved if there are specific issues to be discussed. (These roles will be discussed in more detail in Chapter 4.) During these scoping meetings it is important to gather all the information necessary to write the project proposal, including:

- **Timescales**
  - When must the application be delivered by?
  - What intermediate milestones are there?

- **Budget**
  - How much is the client willing to pay?
  - How much will they pay up-front?
  - Will interim payments be made?
  - How will satisfactory completion be judged?

- **Clients' business aims**
  - What is the client hoping the application will achieve: generating sales, raising profile, gathering information, training?
  - What does the client want the application to say about them: traditional, innovative, fun, trustworthy?

- **User aims and motivations**
  - Why will the user be using the application: to find information, for pleasure, for work, to learn new skills?
  - How often will they use the application: once only, daily, weekly?

- **User characteristics**
  - What can be said in general terms about the users: age, spending power, familiarity with computers, education, language, culture?
  - Will they be given training to use the application?
  - Are they familiar with any existing systems on which we can model the new application?

- **Delivery platform**
  - Are there any constraints placed on the design: old hardware, limited network bandwidth, information kiosk, CD-ROM delivery?

- **Media composition**
  - What mix of media does the client want: text, graphics, animations, audio, video?
  - Is it practical given the delivery platform?
  - What media already exist that can be reused: corporate videos, advertising jingles, company reports, existing Web site?

The scoping meetings also give the clients the opportunity to ask questions. If the client has not already seen the developers' portfolio of work, then this can be presented to the clients.

Alongside the scoping meetings, the business manager may also be conducting market analysis, examining the clients' competitors and trends in the clients' business area.

The creative team may be preparing overall treatments and mock-ups of design ideas, while the technical team identify appropriate technologies and technical approaches.

On the basis of all the information gathered, the project manager must assess the overall feasibility of the clients' proposal – can it be produced by the deadline, can it be produced given the budget, does the development team possess the necessary skills and experience to complete the development successfully? If the project manager is convinced of the development's feasibility then they produce a project plan and a budget.

Proposal document

A **proposal document** and possibly a presentation are then produced. The proposal document is important because it will form the basis of the contract with the client. It must provide a clear, unambiguous description of the overall approach that will be followed, the different factors which have led to the proposed approach, a project plan and budget outline. At this stage in the development process there will be many things that aren't yet known, so we may wish to list alternatives or potential approaches. The proposal is likely to require input from both the technical and creative teams under the leadership of the project manager and business manager. The proposal document should include:

- **Client requirements** – a statement of the clients' business aims.

- **User requirements** – a statement of user characteristics and user aims.

- **Approach** – the overall approach for the application, how it meets client and user requirements, media composition, general look and feel, general content organisation.

- **Project plan** – begin and end dates, intermediate milestones and deliverables.

- **Budget** – how much is to be paid, when it is to be paid, whether the payment is conditional on reaching a milestone or making a deliverable.

- **Client responsibilities** – things which the client agrees to do, e.g. providing existing media for reuse, checking the legal situation regarding their reuse.

- **Exclusions** – things that are explicitly not part of the contract, e.g. maintenance, training.

A presentation to the client is important as it gives the client an impression of the developers as well as the proposal itself. This can be particularly important if the bidding process is a competitive one. The business manager or project manager may give the presentation, probably with support from the creative and technical team leaders.

If the proposal is successful, there is likely to be some final contract negotiation, a finalisation of the budget and delivery milestones and other legal agreements, all involving the legal advisors. Once this is completed, the development stage begins.

Development

The development stage is where the developers take their initial creative and technical ideas and put them into practice. The end result of this stage is a complete application. A number of the tools and techniques we might use during this stage are examined in Chapter 6.

The development phase begins with requirements analysis, though some initial analysis may have been done during the bidding stage in preparation for the proposal document. Requirements analysis refers to a variety of activities that are performed in order to discover the requirements of the application.

- **User analysis** – aims, motivations, characteristics. We need to recognise that there are different types of users, not just end users, but also administrators and managers.

- **Task analysis** – what tasks does the application need to support, how quickly must they be done, how accurately must they be done, will they be done by individuals or in groups?

- **Environment analysis** – where will the application be located? If the environment is noisy or dirty it may affect our design.

- **System analysis** – the hardware and supporting software requirements. It may be that due to the environment, a touch screen is a better solution than a keyboard and mouse. Our design may be restricted by the hardware platform that the application has to run on, or the way in which it is to be delivered.

- **Competitor analysis** – what similar applications already exist, what are they doing that is good or bad?

We must also consider any **non-functional requirements** such as safety, security, performance, capacity, reliability, usability, quality and maintainability.

We will use a variety of techniques to gather the application requirements, including interviews with potential users and observation of existing systems and users.

Creative, technical and content design

On the basis of this analysis, the creative and technical design of the application can be developed. It is important to remember that the creative and technical aspects of the application cannot be considered in isolation, as both will place demands and limitations on the other. The project manager must ensure that communication between the creative and technical teams takes place.

The creative team will be focusing on a range of design issues, the overall look and feel, page layouts, interactivity, icon design and so on. The technical team will be looking at alternative technical solutions, performance issues, usability, implementation and so on. Content creation and preparation will be taking place along with information architecture activities concerned with the way content should be structured and organised.

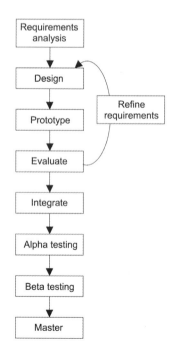

Figure 3.5 Development stage

Creative, technical and content designs will all need to be tested with users. Designs will evolve and requirements cannot be precisely known in advance. We want to make any major changes at the beginning of the process, with the changes getting smaller and smaller through the process. The development stage should therefore be **user-centred** (focused on real users and their tasks and involving users in the design process through the development and evaluation of designs) and iterative.

Evaluation

Each design needs to be mocked-up as a **prototype** and **evaluated**. Ideally this evaluation will be with users, but this can be impracticable and expensive to do for every single design decision. We may instead evaluate with members of the development team who have not been involved in the design, or with other company staff. In some cases we will actually want to evaluate with the clients, for example to see if the look and feel of the design fits with their corporate identity. After the evaluation we should be in a position to decide if the design needs to be changed or if our requirements need to be refined. If the refinement of the requirements is likely to increase the costs of the development, we will ask the clients whether they want to pay the increased costs, or follow the original requirements. The evaluation and possible refinement of requirements may lead to a redesign, which again will need to be prototyped and evaluated.

It may be necessary to repeat this **iterative cycle** (Figure 3.6) several times before a final design is arrived at. The type of prototype we build and the type of evaluation we conduct is going to depend greatly on the type of design we are evaluating and what it is we want to know about the design.

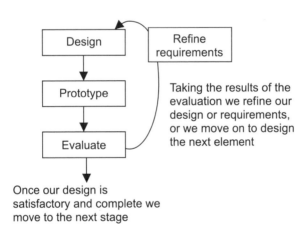

Figure 3.6 The iterative cycle

CRUCIAL TIP

The **iterative cycle** really captures the whole essence of the design process and is central to the development process as a whole. It is important to understand what it is and why it is used.

Implementation

This iterative process will be followed by an integration phase, resulting in a complete implementation of the application. This **alpha version** can then be used for internal testing using mock users within the development company – ideally not people who have been directly involved in the development. When any problems found with the alpha version have been fixed, a **beta version** can then be released to selected users. It is important that these beta testers have not been involved with the development process so that they can provide an objective, unbiased view. When any problems identified by the beta testers have been fixed, a final **master copy** of the application is produced. This master copy will be used for making copies in the case of a CD-ROM, installed on a Web server in the case of a Web site, or installed on the delivery platform in the case of software.

Launch

The launch stage is where the completed application is delivered to the users. Some of the activities in this stage, such as marketing or packaging, may be carried out by the clients or by other specialists. The end result of this stage is a complete application in actual use by users.

The first activity is **archiving** the whole project, which should be done by the developers. This involves careful storage and indexing of all the design documentation, media, code and so on that have been generated during the development, as well as the final application. The project manager should write an end of development review, highlighting any aspects of the development from which lessons can be learned. It is also useful to keep a record of the actual costs incurred as this can be used as a guide for setting future project budgets. If archiving is done effectively it can serve as a useful resource for future developments, both in terms of building on good practice, but also possibly in terms of reusing media or design ideas. It is also useful for a development company to keep an overall index of the different projects and their resources for the same reasons.

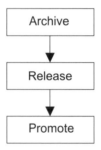

Figure 3.7 Launch stage

The **release** or launching of the application is likely to involve a combination of different activities. If the application is a Web site it will involve configuring the Web server and installing the site. If it is a CD-ROM it will involve making copies from the master, packaging and distributing it to sales outlets. If it is a stand-alone information kiosk then it will involve installation at the site or delivery to the clients.

Promotion may or may not be necessary depending on the nature of the application. For a Web site this may involve registration with search engines, having the site reviewed in magazines or review Web sites, or having the site listed in specialist directories. For a CD-ROM it may involve advertising in traditional media, having the application reviewed in appropriate magazines or review Web sites, or installing window displays and other promotional material in retail outlets. For the more specialist marketing activities it is likely that a marketing company will be employed, but registration with search engines and specialist directories may well be part of the developers' remit. Appropriate search engines and directories would have been identified in the bidding or development stage.

Maintenance

For many developments the development process ends with the launch stage. For others, particularly Web sites, there is an important additional stage – maintenance. The maintenance stage allows for the fact that applications will often need to be modified after completion. An application may need to be modified for a number of reasons, including:

- content becomes out of date, is not used, or new content needs to be added;
- the business needs of the clients change;
- the needs or expectations of the users change;
- new technology is available;
- design becomes dated.

Updating and adding content and fixing minor bugs takes place in the **maintenance** activity.

Evolution involves larger scale changes, perhaps the addition of new functionality, addition or removal of whole sections of content, or the incorporation of new technologies. Evolution takes place within the existing application design, extending rather than replacing it.

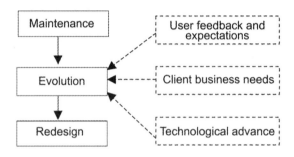

Figure 3.8 Maintenance stage

Eventually it is likely that an application cannot be extended further, perhaps it has become too complicated, has become fragmented due to too much evolution, or can no longer reflect client or user needs. At this point a **redesign** is necessary. This will essentially involve going through the complete development lifecycle again. Although we will have previously gathered a large quantity of information about the clients, users, the market and so on, we will need to do this all again as all these things will have changed. It may be that we can reuse some of the media, design elements, or technology in the redesigned application, though this will depend on how well the initial development was archived and indexed.

Quick test

1. What information will be gathered at a scoping meeting?

2. What information is included in a project proposal?

3. What is the iterative cycle and in which stage does it occur?

Section 3

End of chapter assessment

Multiple choice questions

1. The four stages of the development lifecycle are –
   a) design, evaluate, refine requirements, prototype
   b) bidding, design, evaluate, launch
   c) scoping meetings, prototype, launch, maintenance
   d) bidding, development, launch, maintenance.

2. The scoping meetings take place between –
   a) developers and users
   b) users, clients and developers
   c) clients and users.
   d) clients and developers.

3. The sequence of events in the iterative cycle are –
   a) design, evaluate, refine requirements, prototype
   b) design, prototype, evaluate, refine requirements
   c) refine requirements, prototype, design, evaluate
   d) prototype, design, evaluate, refine requirements.

Multiple choice answers

1. d) is the right answer (see Figure 3.3).

2. d) is the right answer. b) could also be right, but it would be unusual to include users at this stage of the development.

3. b) is the right answer (see Figure 3.6).

Questions

1. Explain why communication is important in the multimedia development process and identify who should be communicating with whom during the four main stages of the development lifecycle.

2. Identify the types of requirements analyses that will be conducted when designing a multimedia application. Give examples of each type.

3. Describe the iterative cycle and explain why it is important in multimedia developments.

4. You have been invited to bid for a project to create a tourist information kiosk to be situated in your local high street. You are about to have your first scoping meeting with the clients. Write an initial set of questions that you will ask.

5. The maintenance stage of the development lifecycle consists of three activities, name them and explain what happens during each of them.

Answers

1. We are being asked to *explain why communication is important* and *identify who should be communicating with whom* and *when*. We are also given a reminder that there are four main stages in the development lifecycle.

The three important sets of people are the developers, the clients and the users. We should also define what these terms mean. Figure 3.2 would be relevant to our answer and helps form the outline of our explanation. We need to explain why these people need to communicate – essentially we need to understand what the users want, and neither the developers nor the clients are likely to have a full understanding of their needs.

In terms of the four stages:

- Bidding will generally involve the clients and developers, communication during scoping meetings is important so that the developers understand the clients' requirements and the clients understand what the developers are proposing. The project proposal is an important piece of communication because it forms the basis of the contract.

- Communication in the development stage will be between the developers and the clients, but most importantly between the developers and the users (we can bring in the notion of user-centred design). Requirements analysis will involve communication with the clients. The iterative cycle (which we should define) involves communication with users and possibly clients through evaluation. This is a critical element in the development process.

- Launch generally involves communication with the users in terms of promotion and marketing.

- Maintenance involves communication with clients and users in terms of changing requirements, feedback and so on.

2. We are being asked to *identify the types of requirements analysis* and to *give examples*.

- User analysis is performed to understand the important characteristics of the users. Depending on the nature of the application we are developing, we may be interested in their aims, motivations, age, education, familiarity with computers, whether they have special needs, their culture.

- Task analysis is performed to understand the tasks the application need to support. What are the tasks, how quickly do users needs to do the tasks, how accurately must they be done, how often will they be done?

- Environment analysis considers where the application will be located. Is the environment noisy or dirty, will the application get a lot of use, is it likely to be vulnerable to theft or damage?

- System analysis examines the hardware and software requirements. The environment analysis or other analyses may place restrictions on the hardware solution that is appropriate. The hardware may also be restricted by the software or vice versa.

- Competitor analysis evaluates existing similar applications in order to learn from what they are doing.

We could also add information about the way in which we would gather these requirements, though we don't look at this until Chapter 6.

3. We are being asked to *describe the iterative cycle* and *explain its importance*. The iterative cycle is shown in Figure 3.6 and ideally we will reproduce this in our answer. The important things that it shows are the four events – design, prototype, evaluate, refine requirements – and the order in which they occur. The other key aspect is that it is iterative – we may go round the cycle several times before our evaluation indicates that our design is satisfactory. We should also place the iterative cycle within the overall context of the development lifecycle.

The importance of the iterative cycle can be explained mainly in terms of communication. The developers and clients are likely to have only a partial understanding of the users. An iterative cycle allows us to test our design with the users and to get feedback on those designs. This helps us to refine our designs and eliminate those that do not meet the users' needs. It can also be helpful to evaluate our ideas with clients to make sure that they are happy with the elements of our design which affect them – for instance the way we are portraying their company on a Web site. If we did not adopt the iterative cycle we could waste time and money developing applications that clients were not happy with and users would not use or buy.

4. We are being asked to *write an initial set of questions for a scoping meeting*. We also need to consider the scenario that we have been given – we looked at some of the issues surrounding public access applications in Chapter 1. These included the need to attract the users' attention; the user just wants to be able to walk up to it and use it. We may need to cater for a wide variety of different users and the user is unlikely to spend very long using the application. As the application will be placed in the street, we also need to consider the appropriate hardware solution – perhaps a touch screen.

   Whilst there is no definitive list of correct questions to ask, we should be asking questions in the seven main areas identified in this chapter:

   - Timescales. When must the application be delivered by?
   - Budget. How much is the client willing to pay? How will satisfactory completion be judged?
   - Clients' business aims. What is the client hoping the application will achieve? What does the client want the application to say about them? What attractions do they want to promote? Does it need to tie in with existing promotional material?
   - User aims and motivations. Why will users be using the application, what information do they need?
   - User characteristics. Who is the application targeted at? What is already known about the tourists, what countries are they from, what do we know about the users: age, spending power, familiarity with computers, education, language, culture?
   - Delivery platform. How many installations will there be? Are there any restrictions on the type of hardware and software that can be used? Would the clients consider a touch screen application?
   - Media composition. What mix of media does the client want: text, graphics, animations, audio, video? What media already exist that can be reused?

   We may also want to clarify whether or not the client wants us to maintain and update the application.

   We should also mention that this is only our initial set of questions and we would expect the answers to these questions to raise more questions in turn. We would then arrange another meeting to discuss these with the clients.

5. We are being asked to *name the activities* and *explain what they involve*. We should start by explaining where the maintenance stage comes in the context of the overall development lifecycle. We know there are three activities from the question – maintenance, evolution and redesign.

   - Maintenance involves updating content, fixing minor bugs, and adding new content. We could mention that this is often done by clients, but that this may lead to problems.
   - Evolution involves larger scale changes, new functionality, major changes in the

content or the addition of new technologies. These changes may be caused by user feedback or changing clients' needs. The changes take place within the existing application design.

- Redesign occurs when an application cannot be extended further and no longer meets users' or clients' needs. This essentially involves a complete redesign from the beginning of the development lifecycle.

We may also mention that maintenance is often not budgeted for by clients and that poor maintenance can lead to a loss of quality for the application over time.

Section 4

Further reading and research

Reading

England, E. and Finney, A. (2002) *Managing Multimedia, Book 1 – People and Processes*, Addison Wesley. Particularly Chapters 3, 4, 5, 6 and 12.
Garrett, J.J. (2002) *The Elements of User Experience*, New Riders.
Goto, K. and Cotler, E. (2002) *Web Redesign: Workflow that Works*, New Riders.

Research

Look for other descriptions of the development lifecycle in books or on the Web. Identify similarities and differences between them and consider whether you would add anything to the lifecycle presented in this chapter for use in your own developments.

Chapter 4
Multimedia
development team

Chapter summary

In this chapter we look at the different roles and skills that are needed within the project team and the crucial role of the project manager. We take a more detailed look at two areas relating to project management – legal issues and budgeting.

Learning outcomes

After studying this chapter you should aim to achieve these targets by answering the questions at the end of the chapter. You should be able to:

> **Outcome 1: Identify the variety of different team roles that may be involved with an application development.**
>
> **Outcome 2: Understand the responsibilities of the project manager and the skills they require.**
>
> **Outcome 3: Demonstrate an awareness of the legal issues in multimedia application development.**
>
> **Outcome 4: Adopt a realistic approach to budgeting a multimedia application development.**

How will you be assessed on this?

In an exam you might be asked to describe the different roles and skills required within a multimedia development team, or to specify the skills needed for a given application development. Because of the importance of the project manager's role, you may also be asked to describe the particular skills they need. This can be related back to the challenges in managing multimedia developments discussed in Chapter 3.

Copyright is very important in multimedia. You may be asked to identify the main points of copyright law – what the rights are, who owns them, how to use copyrighted material and so on.

In group coursework that asked you to build a multimedia application, you may be required to fulfil a particular role or roles. In an individual coursework the different roles serve as a useful reminder of the aspects that need to be considered in the project plan and budget. You will almost certainly need to consider the issue of copyright in any coursework.

CRUCIAL TIP

If you intend to use copyright material (or material with uncertain copyright status) in an assignment you should check with your lecturer as to what is appropriate.

CRUCIAL TIP

Because copyright will have an influence on every multimedia development and media type, knowledge about copyright can be used in answering examination questions on a wide variety of multimedia topics.

Section 1

The project team

In this section we examine the key skills and roles required by the multimedia development team. Whilst many of these roles will be common to the majority of developments, it will often be necessary to bring in specialists for a particular development.

CRUCIAL CONCEPTS

The **multimedia development team** requires a variety of different knowledge and skills. These can be grouped into four areas: **business and administrative**; **creative**; **technical**; and **specialist**. The **project manager** is vital for ensuring that a development is successful.

Given the diversity of potential applications and the characteristics of multimedia development, a multimedia project team will require a variety of different skills. The precise blend of skills required will depend on the particular application being developed and will vary throughout the different stages of the development process. In some cases an individual member of the team will have a number of different skills that are appropriate to the development process and will in effect combine several roles.

Often applications will be making use of new technology and team members will be learning the technology during the development process. This can lead to increased strain on team members and make it difficult to plan how long development activities will take. Specialist team members may be shared between several development projects, again putting pressure on deadlines.

All of these difficulties need to be managed to reduce their impact, along with all the usual pressures due to deadlines, budgets, staff illness, friction within the development team, etc. The project manager is therefore central to the success of a multimedia development.

Whilst much of the work will be done in-house by existing employees, there may be no one in the team who has a required skill or the required technical facilities may not be available. This means that it may be necessary to hire additional staff on a contract basis. This decision needs to be made early on in negotiations with the clients so that any external contractors can be properly budgeted for.

The roles involved in a typical multimedia development can be grouped into four main areas (Figure 4.1). The figure shows an extended project team; in practice few projects will have such a large team and a minimal **core project team** is also shown.

Business and administrative roles

It is important to recognise that multimedia development is a business, and that design and implementation can only be successful if it is well managed and well supported in terms of administrative functions.

Project manager

The role of project manager is the key to a successful development. They are responsible for ensuring that the development is completed to a satisfactory standard, by the agreed deadline and within budget. They are involved in the scoping and definition of the application with the client, producing the project plan and budget. They are responsible for assembling the other team members and making sure they have the necessary resources and skills to work effectively and according to the plan and budget. They will need a variety of communication, interpersonal and managerial skills to ensure effective teamwork, in particular to aid communication between the technical and creative teams.

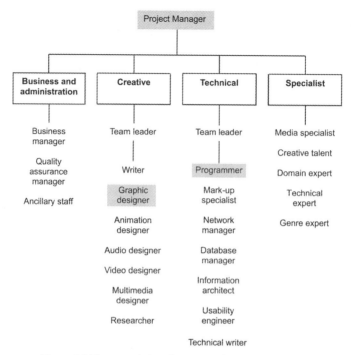

Figure 4.1 The extended project tream (core team in grey)

Business manager

The business manager acts as the liaison between the client and the development company, defining the business requirements of the application. This will often be a long-term relationship involving the definition of a business strategy for the client and the development and maintenance of a number of different applications. They may also be responsible for analysing the state of the market and business and consumer trends. The project manager will often fill this role.

Quality assurance manager

The quality assurance manager is responsible for making sure that the application meets the criteria identified in the scoping document and adheres to the results of the requirements analysis. They are responsible for the creation and execution of test plans and may also co-ordinate usability testing. They need to communicate the findings to the other team members so that problems can be rectified. They may be responsible for applying other quality assurance policies adopted by the development company, for instance, regarding the budgeting and accounting procedures. The project manager will often fill this role.

Ancillary staff

There are a number of supporting roles which may not always be seen as part of the development team but which play an important part in the successful completion of a project. In larger development companies these may be in-house staff, otherwise they will be contracted in on an as-needed basis. The ancillary staff includes those involved in clerical support, marketing, packaging design and legal advice.

Creative roles

The creative team is responsible for the preparation of the multimedia content and also for the overall look and feel of the application.

Team leader

If the project team is sufficiently large, the creative team will often have their own team leader. This team leader is responsible for managing the creative aspects of the project and the creative staff. They will also be responsible for the overall design concept of the application. They operate under the overall management of the project manager.

Writer

The writer is responsible for the text content of the site, creating original content, writing scripts for video and audio content and editing and proof reading content produced by others. They are also responsible for setting the overall 'voice' of the application and checking for consistency and style.

Graphic designer

The graphic designer is responsible for the visual look and feel of the application. This will include the layout of pages, the design of graphical elements, such as buttons and icons, and choosing the colour scheme. They will also be responsible for producing content graphics and working with digitised photographs. (See also Chapter 8.)

Animation designer

The animation designer is responsible for the design and production of animations within the application. The graphic designer may handle simple animations, such as button rollover effects. More complex animations and content animations may require the specialist skills of the animation designer. The animation designer may be a contracted media specialist, rather than a regular member of the team. (See also Chapter 9.)

Audio designer

The audio designer is responsible for the design and production of audio within the application. They may be involved in all stages, scripting, capturing the raw sound, digitising it, editing it, and preparing the final files to be incorporated into the application. Where sophisticated audio is necessary, perhaps requiring a full recording studio, the audio design work may be a contracted media specialist. (See also Chapter 10.)

Video designer

The video designer is responsible for the design and production of video for the application. Producing video for multimedia application places different constraints on the designer than those faced in television or cinema and the video designer needs to have experience in working within these constraints. Straightforward footage may be produced in-house, with the video designer involved in all stages, storyboarding, scripting, filming, digitising, editing and preparing the final files to be incorporated into the application. The production of more complex or professional footage is likely to be contracted out to a media specialist, though the editing and preparation of the final files is still likely to be conducted in-house. (See also Chapter 11.)

Multimedia designer

The multimedia designer specialises in the effective combination of different media, interactivity, metaphors and navigation. They will work closely with the other members of the creative team and may also work closely with the technical team in order to implement their designs. (See also Chapter 5.)

Researchers

Researchers are responsible for researching subject content appropriate to the application and identifying and locating specific existing media elements that are needed. They may also be responsible for identifying domain experts and copyright holders.

Technical roles

The technical team are responsible for designing, building and testing the implementation of the application. They will often be working from the ideas produced by the creative team. Some aspects, such as database design, are less likely to have this creative input, but will instead be based on the technical requirements as identified during the requirements analysis.

Team leader
As with the creative team, the technical team will often have their own team leader.

Programmers
A number of different types of programming may be required for a multimedia application, including authoring and scripting using an authoring package, writing applets and implementing databases.

Mark-up specialists
These specialise in the use of mark-up languages, such as HTML, XML or WML. They may also be responsible for the development of CSSs and DTDs (see Chapters 12 and 13 for an explanation of these terms).

Network manager
A network manager is responsible for setting up and configuring networks and servers (email servers, Web servers, streaming media servers etc.). This role may continue on a contract basis after the completion of the application development, the clients may take on the role themselves, or it may be passed to a third party such as a Web hosting service.

Database manager
A database manager is responsible for the design and maintenance of database systems. Databases play an increasingly important role in many multimedia applications, particularly Web-based applications which have a database back-end in which content is held. This role may also continue on a contract basis after the application development, the clients may take on the role themselves, or it may be passed to a third party.

Information architect
An information architect specialises in the overall organisation of content within an application and how the user navigates through that content. They are also concerned with how to label and describe content and how to facilitate effective searching and browsing.

Usability engineer
A usability engineer will advise on the design and implementation of the application from the perspective of how usable it is. This will also involve planning and conducting a variety of usability evaluations, often with users.

Technical writers
Whilst for many small-scale applications there will be little or no need to produce user guides and technical documentation, for larger systems such documentation will certainly be required. A technical writer needs to communicate technical information clearly, concisely and in a way that makes sense to the reader.

Specialist roles

Specialists are typically brought in on a contract basis to meet the needs of a particular application development. They have in-depth knowledge of a specific area or a particular creative talent that is not generally required for all multimedia applications or which cannot be financially justified on a full-time basis.

Media specialists

Media specialists are experts in some aspect of media production – they may for example be audio or video engineers, photographers, animators or 3D modellers. Their skills are typically more specialised than those of the creative team.

Creative talent

Actors, musicians, composers and similar creative talent may be required when producing the media elements for the application.

Experts

Experts can be divided into three main types, **domain experts** who possess in-depth knowledge about a subject area and provide content for the application; **technology experts** who have technical knowledge and experience in using specific technologies, such as media streaming or solving a particular technical issue such as localisation (converting a multimedia application from one language to another); and **genre experts** who have experience in developing particular types of application; an instructional designer may be used for an educational application, whilst a specialist games designer may be used when developing an application which involves some element of game play.

CRUCIAL TIP

As well as naming the different roles, you should be able to describe the skills required. Remember also that a team member may fill several roles.

Quick test

1. The roles involved in a typical multimedia development can be grouped into four main areas – what are they?

2. Which role is the key to a successful development?

3. Why are specialists generally not part of the in-house development team?

Section 2

Project management issues

In this section we examine two aspects of application development in more detail – legal issues and budgeting. Both these issues are critical in application development and they are related to each other, as the costs associated with obtaining copyright licences may be significant.

Although the project manager will typically have a team that provide advice, the project manager generally has the final word. Because of this, the project manager needs to have some understanding of all the aspects of application development.

Legal issues

CRUCIAL CONCEPTS

There are a number of **legal issues** surrounding multimedia development, arguably the most important are those concerning **Intellectual Property Rights (IPR)**. **Copyright** is the key IPR for multimedia as it protects the work we create and applies to the work of others that we might want to use.

45

There are a number of issues relating to contracts, confidentiality and commercial sensitivity, which we will not look at here, even though they do impact upon the development. Instead we will consider Intellectual Property Rights (IPRs). IPRs are covered by a number of different laws, design laws relating to the design of aesthetic and functional articles, trade marks relating to branded goods and services, patents covering inventions and copyright covering creative works. Here we will focus on the key IPR for multimedia – copyright.

===================================== CRUCIAL TIP =====================================

Remember that IPR law varies between countries. Make sure any reading or research you do relates to UK law.

Copyright applies to several general categories of work all of which are subject to broad interpretation. Any piece of work that is **created** in a **tangible form** (e.g. written down, drawn, stored on CD-ROM) and is **not a direct copy** of another work is potentially copyrighted. Those works that are particularly relevant to multimedia include:

- **literary works** – including text, software, manuals and databases;
- **musical works** – including songs, jingles and lyrics;
- **pictorial and graphic works** – including photographs, graphics and drawings;
- **audio-visual works** – including films and TV programmes;
- **audio recordings** – including music, sounds and words.

The **copyright owner** controls a number of **rights**, including:

- **reproduction right** – copying the work;
- **modification right** – modifying a work to create a new work;
- **distribution right** – distributing copies.

Some works also have '**moral rights**' which are designed to protect an author's reputation.

Anyone who exercises any of these rights without the permission of the copyright holder is violating copyright and may be liable to pay damages and to deliver up the infringing materials to the copyright holder.

The creator of a work generally owns the copyright, so it is important to identify who the author is. For some forms of media (such as text) this is relatively easy, the situation with other media (such as a sound recording) can be more complex. If the author creates the work as part of their employment, the employer generally owns the copyright. When a self-employed contractor creates a work, the copyright resides with the contractor unless it is explicitly transferred to the company. Therefore we must be careful when using specialists on a contract basis, as we (or our client) will typically want to hold the copyright. The multimedia development company will typically own the copyright to the multimedia application and any media we create, though this may be transferred to the client as part of the terms of the contract.

Licences for any or all of these rights can be agreed under a wide variety of terms and conditions. The transfer or sale of ownership of a copyright is also possible. When we wish to use copyrighted media in our applications we need to consider whether we wish to buy the copyright outright or just license certain rights. If we wish to have an **exclusive licence** (so other people cannot use the same media for the duration of the licence), the cost will increase. Budgeting for licences is an important part of project management. Special types of licence are required in some circumstances, for example to synchronise sound with images. The complexity of gaining copyright licences has led to many developers using only original, in-house material. When creating in-house material we must remember that actors, models and narrators own the rights to recorded material in which they perform, regardless of whether or not they are professional. It is important to ensure that they sign an appropriate **release form** to transfer the rights.

The **duration** of a copyright is complicated by a variety of factors, including the copyright law that existed at the time a work was created, copyright extensions available under previous copyright laws, the type of work and so on. Generally copyright lasts for the term of the author's life, plus 70 years after their death.

Once copyright expires, or if the holder relinquishes the copyright to a work, it is said to be in the **public domain**. Such works can be used by anyone, for any purpose, without cost and without the need to obtain any licence.

Copyright law does allow some limited use of copyright material without the copyright holder's permission under '**fair dealing**' (often referred to as 'fair use'). This area of the law is rather vague and it is unlikely to apply to a commercial multimedia application.

CRUCIAL TIP

Your learning resources centre may have collections of copyright free material, or material for which a licence has been obtained. This can be used in an assignment without the need to obtain further permissions. Always check that the terms of any licence allow you to use the media the way you want to.

Budgeting

CRUCIAL CONCEPTS

Setting and **adhering** to a **budget** isn't easy for multimedia developments, but is essential to its success and is an important part of the project manager's role. The budget identifies **items** that must be paid for, their **cost**, and recognises that **costs may increase**.

Budgeting for a multimedia application development is difficult for a variety of reasons, including:

- The exact details of the application are not fully known at the time the budget is written – some will only become apparent during the development process.
- The number of prototypes and evaluations is hard to predict.
- All developments are different, so it is hard to generalise from past experience.
- Standard models for the costs are not available.
- Costs for copyright licensing can be hard to estimate.
- Failure to understand client or user requirements can result in costly mistakes.
- Clients may underestimate the cost of multimedia development as they are not familiar with the process.
- Failure to fully appreciate the cost of maintenance.

Initial failure to set an appropriate budget or failure to adhere to a budget can result in a poor final project. The setting and managing of the budget is one of the project manager's most important tasks.

Essentially setting the budget consists of three stages: identifying items that must be paid for, determining how much they will cost, and allowing for factors that may cause these costs to increase.

The items that must be paid for include:

- team members;
- additional specialists brought in on a contract basis;
- talent, such as actors or musicians;

- software, upgrades, maintenance;
- hardware and equipment, upgrades, maintenance;
- consumables, paper, CD-ROMs, ink cartridges, phone calls, postage;
- copyright licences or purchases;
- payment of test subjects during evaluations;
- travel costs to visit clients;
- the cost of project management and administration.

The cost estimates for these should be based on the costs incurred during previous projects, current market rates and so on. It is also important to try to accurately estimate the time that different activities will take. Again this can be based on experience in previous projects.

Factors that may increase costs include:

- hardware, software or equipment failure;
- time taken to learn new software;
- revisions asked for by client;
- number of prototypes built and evaluated.

Where possible these unpredictable costs need to be budgeted for and controlled. We may set a limit in the contract on the number of revisions the client can ask for without incurring additional costs. Once the budget has been set, the project manager must track expenditure against the budget.

Quick test

1. What types of work are protected by copyright?
2. What rights does the copyright holder control?
3. Why is it difficult to budget accurately for a multimedia development?

Section 3

End of chapter assessment

Multiple choice questions

1. If a development team doesn't contain anyone with the specialist skill to create part of the application, the best option is to –

   a) train a member of the team
   b) redesign the application so it doesn't use that media type
   c) employ an external specialist
   d) do the best with the existing team skills.

2. It is legal to use copyright material without permission in an application, so long as you acknowledge the source –

   a) always true
   b) always false
   c) it depends on whether you will make money from the application
   d) it depends if the material is on the Web

e) it depends how the material is used.

3. If a self-employed contractor creates a media element for a multimedia development company, the copyright of that media is held by –

a) the development company
b) the project manager
c) the contractor
d) the client.

Multiple choice answers

1. This is a trick question. Any of the answers could be right depending on the application, the budget, how important the part of the application is, how difficult it would be to master the skills, how much time is available. These are the types of judgements that a project manager has to make.

2. e) is the right answer, it may be possible to use the material if it can be considered 'fair dealing' (this will not generally apply to multimedia applications). c) and d) make no difference at all.

3. c) is the right answer, unless the contract specifies otherwise. Normally we would transfer these rights to the development company or the client in the contract.

Questions

1. You are project manager for a small-scale development project. The application is a CD-ROM prospectus and promotion for a university which will be sent to schools. In addition to your project management skills, identify the skills and knowledge your project team will require.

2. Describe the typical tasks that a project manager will be responsible for and identify some of the skills it is necessary for them to possess.

3. A multimedia development team plans to include a video clip in an information kiosk they are creating to promote a company at a trade show. Currently they are considering three options: digitising an existing promotional video of the company; creating new video footage with actors; finding an appropriate video clip on the Web and using it. Identify the potential legal issues that the development team should be aware of when considering each of the options.

4. You are negotiating the budget with a client who wants a precise prediction of the costs of prototyping that will be incurred during the development. Outline the key points of your argument as to why this is not possible and suggest some form of compromise.

Answers

1. We are being asked to *identify the skills and knowledge needed in the project team*. We also need to consider the scenario that we have been given – we have been told that it is a small-scale project, so we are unlikely to have a large budget. We also know that it will be delivered on CD-ROM, so we know that we don't need a network manager. We can also assume that much of the media we will need already exists, for example in the paper-based prospectus. We may also wish to make other assumptions. This is fine, so long as we state what our assumptions are.

In addition to listing the skills and knowledge we will require and explaining why we need them, we can also list the skills that we do not require. If we follow the list given in Section 1:

49

- Project manager – although the question mentions project management skills we may still want to identify them. We might include budgeting, planning, people management, knowledge of multimedia applications.

- Business manager – because this is a small-scale project the project manager is likely to be responsible for the client/developer relationship, understanding and analysing the market place.

- Quality assurance manager – again this role is likely to be filled by the project manager who will need to check that standards are adhered to and procedures followed.

- Ancillary staff – we are likely to require someone with legal knowledge, but the other administrative functions can be carried out by the project manager.

- Creative team leader – because it is a small project, the project manager can assume this role. They will be responsible for the overall design concept. If they do not have training in this area, they may defer some of the responsibility to the graphic designer.

- Writer – we probably don't need a writer as much of the material will already be written. If we do need some more content, the university should be able to provide us with it.

- Graphic designer – we will require someone with a creative background to help define the overall design concept and to create the graphic elements required.

- Animation designer – there is nothing to suggest that we need an animation specialist. Simple animations can be created by the graphic designer.

- Audio designer – whilst there is likely to be some audio in the application, it is unlikely that it will need a great deal of technical knowledge to create or edit. We may find that the authoring programmer has enough basic knowledge.

- Video designer – it is unclear whether there will be video in the application, though we can assume there will be. It may be that the university already has promotional video, or they may have a media production unit who can produce the video for us. Any simple editing can probably be done by another member of the team, so we are unlikely to need a video specialist.

- Multimedia designer – we require some knowledge of how to combine different media and provide navigation. There does not seem to be a great need for sophisticated interactivity or the use of metaphors. It is likely that the graphic designer and authoring programmer will have enough knowledge to fulfil this role.

- Researchers – as most of the material will already exist, we do not need researchers.

- Technical team leader – because it is a small project, the project manager can assume this role. They will be responsible for the overall technical approach. If they do not have training in this area, they may defer some of the responsibility to the programmers.

- Programmers and mark-up specialists – we need to make some assumptions about how the application will be implemented. Even though it is being delivered on CD-ROM, it could still be implemented as Web pages. So far we have made the assumption that there is an authoring programmer using an authoring tool to create the application. This is a reasonable assumption, but we need to state that we are making it. The authoring programmer will have specialist knowledge about the authoring tool and will be required. As we have already mentioned, they may also be expected to do some basic editing on media elements.

- Network manager and database manager – we can make the assumption that neither of these is required. (If you wished to make the assumption that the application will be driven by a database, then this would also be reasonable.)

- Information architect and usability engineer – whilst we may not want a specialist, we need to make sure that there is knowledge about how to plan and conduct an evaluation and how to gain an understanding of the overall organisation of the content. If the project manager or other team members do not have this knowledge, then someone with this knowledge will be required.

- Technical writers – it is reasonable to assume that there will be no need to provide extensive documentation for the system. Any brief documentation that is required can be produced by other team members.
- Specialist roles – we are unlikely to need specialists. If we require domain experts or creative talent, we can make use of the university staff and students.

Our team for this development (assuming they have the skills identified) is:

- project manager;
- legal advisor (probably contracted-in);
- graphic designer;
- authoring programmer;
- usability engineer (unless the other team members have sufficient knowledge).

2. We are being asked to *describe the typical tasks that a project manager carries out* and *identify the skills they need* in order to do a good job. We can refer back to some of the ideas discussed in Chapter 3 in answering this question. If you have studied project management on another course, you can also draw on that information.

Our answer is likely to include a discussion of:

- Why multimedia projects are difficult to manage, each project is unique, it is hard to adopt a standard development approach.
- The role of project manager in ensuring effective communication between developers and clients, developers and users, and within the development team.
- The project manager is involved in the scoping meetings, writing the project proposal and selling the proposal to the clients.
- The project manager is responsible for the budget and project plan and making sure that the project is delivered on time, under budget and to a high quality (we could reproduce the cost-delivery-quality cube in our answer, see Figure 3.1).
- The project manager selects the project team and decides whether external contractors are required.
- The project manager allocates team members to tasks, and sets deadlines and reviews progress.
- The project manager must deal with any unexpected events, such as staff illness, equipment failure and changing client requirements.
- The project manager is responsible for drawing lessons from application developments so that future developments can be more effective.

The skills they require include:

- good communication skills;
- patience;
- a sense of humour;
- the ability to understand people and get the best out of them;
- attention to detail and accurate record keeping;
- a basic understanding of all aspects of multimedia applications.

You will notice that a number of the skills listed weren't mentioned in this chapter. Many of the skills required are fairly obvious. If they seem reasonable, put them into your answer.

3. We are being asked to *identify the legal issues for each of the three options*. Although this may look like a question on video, it is a question about Intellectual Property Rights. For each of the three options we need to say what the legal issues might be and what we might do to resolve them:

   - Digitising an existing promotional video of the company. This is a good solution if the company owns the IPR. If they don't it may still be worth licensing them from the video company. We may ask for an exclusive licence, or just rely on the fact that no other companies will want to use the footage. If the video company wants to charge a lot for the licence, it may be cheaper to pursue one of the other options. On the other hand, because it has been professionally produced, the quality will be high and the legal issues surrounding its production (releases from actors, use of music) will already have been taken care of.

   - Creating new video footage with actors. Whilst this gives us maximum control over the video, it will also be an expensive option in terms of production costs and possibly in terms of actor releases, licences to use music, and so on. We may also need permission to film in certain locations.

   - Finding an appropriate video clip on the Web and using it. We must be cautious about using material from the Web, even if it says it is copyright free. Often the person making the material available does not have the right to do so. Unless we have a legal document saying that they accept responsibility if it turns out that the material is copyrighted (a liability waiver), it is often best to avoid such material. Even if we are certain that the person does own the rights, we are unlikely to get an exclusive licence. If it is just general footage, this may not matter.

We could also mention the possibility of combining these approaches, using some stock footage, combined with new footage and excerpts from the promotional video. We would need to make sure we had appropriate rights for all the sources though. We might also mention some of the general difficulties in licensing for multimedia applications.

Notice that we have included some information in our answer that was not directly asked for in the question, for example about cost implications. It is good practice to add this additional information provided you also give the information asked for in the question and that you do not stray too far from the point. This is a question about IPR, it would not be appropriate to discuss the different ways we might use a video clip within a multimedia application.

4. We are being asked to *outline our key points* and *suggest some potential compromises*. We can draw on some of the material in Chapter 3 about the iterative cycle and the importance of testing with users. If we don't test with users, then we may end up designing an application that they won't or can't use – this will cost the client money. We can also argue that the client may not have a full understanding of the users' requirements and prototyping helps to refine them. We won't really know what needs to be prototyped until we start designing and evaluating. The value in prototyping is in the quality of the final product.

As a compromise we may agree a fixed budget for a certain number of prototypes, with a review afterwards to discuss the finding and decide if further prototyping is required – subject to the client paying more. We may agree that after a fixed number of prototypes (or a fixed amount has been spent) that prototyping will stop, but the client has to accept that there may still be problems with the application. We may agree to involve the client closely in the prototyping process so that they can see that they are getting value for money.

Section 4

Further reading and research

Reading

Bainbridge, D. (1999) *Introduction to Computer Law*, Longman.

Burdman, J. (1999) *Collaborative Web Development*, Addison Wesley.

England, E. and Finney, A. (2002) *Managing Multimedia, Book 1 – People and Processes*, Addison Wesley. Particularly Chapters 2, 10 and 14 on the project team and project management and Chapters 9 and 15 on legal issues.

The Patent Office (*www.patent.gov.uk*) provides a variety of printed and online material relating to all aspects of intellectual property rights. They also maintain an IPR portal at *www.intellectual-property.gov.uk* which contains useful resources and information.

Research

Research some resources on project management, particularly those relating to the effective management of people. Produce a list of hints and tips that would be useful in the management of a multimedia project.

Investigate the cost of developing a Web site for a small business. Visit development companies' Web sites to find prices. Contact development companies to see if they have price lists for standard developments.

Chapter 5
Multimedia design

Chapter summary

In this chapter we look at the aspects that need to be considered when designing multimedia applications. We start by looking at content selection and chunking. Then we consider how the content chunks can be structured and what navigational aids we will provide the user with. We then look at screen layout, colour, metaphors and interactivity.

Learning outcomes

After studying this chapter you should aim to achieve these targets by answering the questions at the end of the chapter. You should be able to:

Outcome 1: Identify the different aspects of multimedia application design.

Outcome 2: Exercise good judgement in the selection and application of design solutions to specific multimedia applications.

How will you be assessed on this?

In an exam you may be asked to describe the different aspects of multimedia design. You may be presented with a scenario and asked to outline the design approach that you would take.

In coursework that required you to build a multimedia application, you would be expected to demonstrate an understanding of design principles through the effective design of your application. You may also be required to explain and justify why you have designed an application in a particular way.

Section 1

Content

In this section we briefly examine factors that will influence the selection of content for our application. We will also look at how we break this content into 'chunks' suitable for presentation to the user.

CRUCIAL CONCEPTS

Content, in terms of text, images, animations, audio and video, is central to every multimedia application. We must break our content into **coherent chunks** (probably combining several different types of media) for presentation to the user.

When selecting our content there are a number of factors we need to take into account:

- **The purpose of the application** – is it trying to entertain, educate, inform or sell? This will influence the type and depth of content and the way we present it.

- **The users** – their age, knowledge and motivation for using the application. Again this will influence the type, depth and presentation of content.

- **The clients** – they may have a firm view on the type of content they want. This may be in keeping with their corporate image.

- **Our competitors' applications** – we may be interested in providing more content, or similar content but cheaper, or in providing very different content.

- **The type of application** – a user may only use an information kiosk once and for only a minute or so, whilst they may use a Web site frequently for ten minutes per visit. We will need to provide different types of content and different depths of content.

- **Maintenance** – how much effort will be required to keep it up to date. We may try to avoid using content that will age quickly, or we may plan and budget for regular maintenance.

- **Existing media** – if there is existing media that can be reused, we can save time and money. The client may already have promotional videos or pamphlets. However we need to be careful that we don't just end up creating an electronic version of their sales brochure.

In addition to choosing our content, we need to think about how we are going to break it down into 'chunks' and how we are going to link those chunks together to form a structure through which the user can navigate.

A **chunk** is a coherent block of content – we will typically think in terms of screens or pages. Each chunk may be composed of a number of different media elements, they are **coherent** in that they relate to the same topic or topics. When deciding how to break our content into chunks, we need to consider:

- **Does it contain too many different topics?** If so we may want to break it into more chunks.

- **Does it contain enough content about the topic or topics?** If not we may want to combine it with another chunk.

- **Does the content fit well within the screen space available?** If there is too much content for the screen space, we may want to break it into smaller chunks.

Quick test

1. How might our competitors' applications influence our content selection?

2. What other factors will influence our selection of content?

3. What is a 'chunk'?

Section 2

Structure

In this section we look at how we can link content chunks into a structure that the user can navigate through. We examine some typical structures and the situations in which they are appropriate.

Chunks of content must be linked together to form a **structure** for the complete application. A good structure is one which comes naturally from a consideration of the content and the users. Common structures are **sequences**, **hierarchies** and **composite** combinations of the two.

Once we have broken our content into chunks, we need to consider how to link those chunks into a structure through which the user can navigate. A **good structure** has the following characteristics:

- it reflects structure that is inherent in the content;
- it represents the users' view of the content, not the clients' or developers';
- it supports the user in their tasks.

If the structure makes sense to the user, they will be able to navigate effectively and carry out their tasks efficiently.

Two of the most common structures are the sequence and the hierarchy. The **sequence**, or **sequential structure**, is an ordered set of chunks, typically supporting 'next' and 'previous' navigation via links or buttons (Figure 5.1).

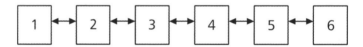

Figure 5.1 Sequential structure

The sequential structure is appropriate when the content needs to be presented to the user in a fixed order. Examples of this include instructions, lessons and stories.

A sequential structure need not be limited to a single path. We may present our user with options, or make a path selection based on user interactions. In Figure 5.2, for example, we may be representing the structure of a story or game where different events happen. On the other hand it could represent some educational package where screen 2 is a test and the user is taken through different content depending on their score.

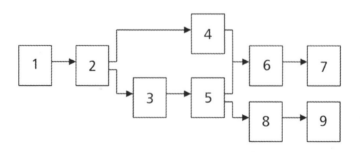

Figure 5.2 Sequential structure with multiple paths

The **hierarchy**, or **hierarchical structure**, groups the chunks into topics, with sub-topics through a series of menus (Figure 5.3). A hierarchy often reflects the natural structure within the content, for instance the internal organisation within a company might be formed of divisions containing departments.

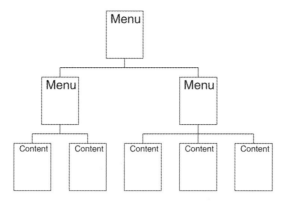

Figure 5.3 Hierarchical structure

When using hierarchies, we need to balance **depth** against **breadth**. If we have a very deep hierarchy (Figure 5.4) the user has to navigate through a large number of short menus before they reach the content.

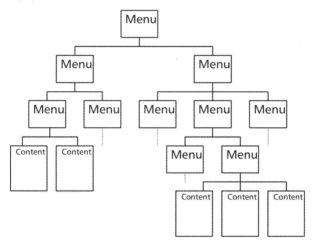

Figure 5.4 Deep hierarchical structure

If we have a very broad hierarchy (Figure 5.5) then the user has to navigate through only a few menus, but each menu has a long list of choices that the user must consider.

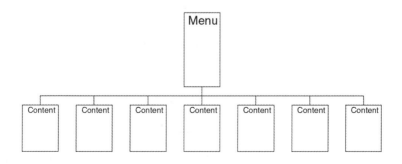

Figure 5.5 Broad hierarchical structure

Often part of our content will be hierarchical and part sequential, for instance a car repair manual may be structured hierarchically in terms of the systems and sub-systems, allowing the user to find the part they are interested in, then sequentially with multiple paths to diagnose the problem and finally sequentially to repair the part (Figure 5.6). This combination of structures is known as a **composite** structure.

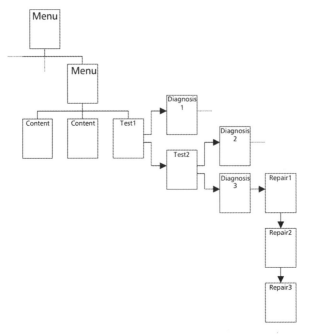

Figure 5.6 Composite structure

Other structures, such as highly interlinked networks and grids, can also be used, but are less common.

Quick test

1. What are the characteristics of a good structure?

2. What are the two most common structures?

3. Are we restricted to using a single structure within an application?

Section 3

Navigation

In this section we examine the characteristics of user navigation and common navigational aids that we might provide for the user.

───────── CRUCIAL CONCEPTS ─────────

The user needs to be able to **navigate** (move) through the **structure** of the application. We can provide users with a number of different **navigational aids** suited to their needs.

Navigation refers to the user moving through the structure of our application. Sometimes this will be directly under the user's control (e.g. picking an option from a menu) and sometimes it will be under the systems control (e.g. based on the user's performance in a quiz). In order to navigate effectively, users need information about:

- where they currently are in the application;
- where they could go next, why they might want to go there and what action they need to perform to go there;
- where they have already been.

When designing our navigation and thinking about navigational aids, it is worth considering the different reasons why a user may be navigating:

- finding out how the navigation aids work;
- browsing around seeing what is available in the application;
- re-orientating themselves if they have become lost in the application;
- seeking a specific piece of information;
- returning to a specific piece of information.

We may need to provide different navigational aids to support each of these activities. We will also need to consider our users. Young children will need something that is simple to use, while adults might require a number of navigation aids for different tasks.

Links and buttons are probably the most common navigational aid. A piece of text or a graphic can be clicked on, taking the user to another screen. Usually we will want to make these obvious to the user and give the user some indication of where the link will take them. Links support browsing and, if a link to the home page or main menu is provided, can help users re-orientate themselves.

Search facilities can be considered a form of navigation and can be quite effective for seeking or returning to a specific piece of information.

Backtracking (Figure 5.7) keeps a list of which screens the user has visited and in which order and then allows the user to move backwards and forwards through the screens on that list (for instance the 'back' and 'forward' buttons on a Web browser). This is useful for returning to a specific piece of information and re-orientation. In addition to using the back and forward buttons, the user may be able to view the list, typically as screen titles, and pick screens directly from it, making it similar to a history list.

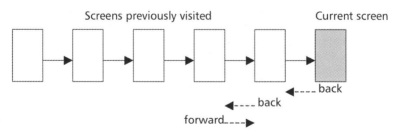

Figure 5.7 Backtracking using 'back' and 'forward'

A **history list** (Figure 5.8) allows users to return directly to previously visited screens without having to retrace their steps. Each previous screen is represented once in the history list, typically by some miniature of the screen or some distinctive graphic. The history list will generally hold only a limited number of previous screens, with older screens being replaced by more recently visited ones. The user is able to return to any of the screens in the history list simply by clicking on it. This is useful for returning to a specific piece of information and re-orientation (we may make a 'main menu' type screen permanently available). A history list is simpler to understand than backtracking, so may be a better choice for young children.

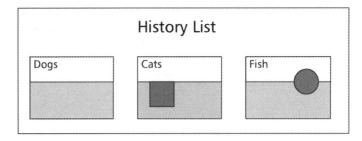

Figure 5.8 History list

A **bookmark list** (Figure 5.9) allows the user to decide which screens they may want to revisit and to add only those to a list. This list then provides some way of identifying the screens (such as a title) and links to those screens. In addition to adding links to the bookmark list, the user may be able to attach annotations or to create sub-lists on specific topics, and move and delete links from the list. A bookmark list is particularly useful for returning to a specific piece of information and also for re-orientation. Because it is under user control, a bookmark list can be far more efficient for a frequent user than backtracking or using a history list.

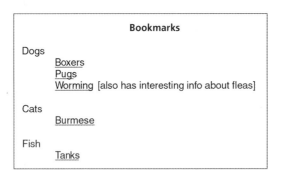

Figure 5.9 Bookmark list with sub-lists and annotation

Overviews and sitemaps (Figure 5.10) provide an overall map of an application, allowing the user to move directly to any part of it. Often this is presented as structured text links, but sometimes as a clickable graphical representation. The user can see what is available, re-orientate themself, and seek and return to a specific piece of information. In large applications it can be difficult to show the entire application, so we may need to provide some form of zoom facility, or a series of maps at different levels of detail.

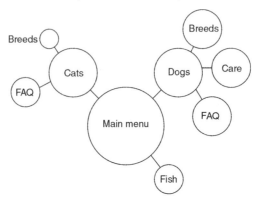

Figure 5.10 Sitemap

We can also use the map to provide the user with other information about the application. In Figure 5.10 for example, the different sizes of the circles could indicate how popular a screen was with users.

Guided tours impose a sequence within the application, based on a topic or perspective about the content. The user can select one of these tours then follow it using 'next' and 'previous' buttons. Although a guided tour can be seen as restricting user navigation, tours can be useful for providing general overviews and task or subject related tours. The user typically has the option to leave a tour at any point and make use of alternative navigational aids.

Whilst we have already said that navigation aids, such as links, should usually be obvious and give an indication where they lead to, this may not always be the case. For particular applications we may wish to disguise the links or make them 'conditional' (available only if certain conditions have been met), perhaps as part of a game.

Quick test

1. For what reasons might a user be navigating an application?

2. Why might a history list be a more suitable navigation aid for young children then a backtrack list?

3. Why might a bookmark list be a more suitable navigation aid for a frequent user than a backtrack list?

Section 4

Screen layout

In this section we discuss the five principles of good page layout and how they can be adapted for designing screen layouts. We also introduce page grids as a tool for designing screen layouts (see also Chapter 6). The use of colour and metaphors are also examined.

CRUCIAL CONCEPTS

The **visual layout** of multimedia applications is particularly important. **Balance, sequence, proportion, emphasis** and **unity** are well established design principles that will help us design our screen layouts. **Colour** is an important part of layout design. We can make our application easier to use by adopting an **interface metaphor**, where we make our application look and behave like something with which the user is already familiar.

The layout of media elements on the screen is an essential consideration in multimedia design. There are already many principles of good layout from the design of paper publications. We can draw on these principles, but we must recognise that multimedia applications have different characteristics and pose different design challenges:

- the size of the screen or page may not be fixed in a multimedia application – particularly if it is being delivered via the Web;
- we need to incorporate navigational elements within the layout, not just content;
- we can use dynamic media (audio, video, animation) within our layout;
- we can move and change elements that are on the screen;
- reading large quantities of text from a computer screen is generally considered tiring;
- the shape of a computer screen is different to that of most paper publications.

Despite these differences, the general principles of balance, sequence, proportion, emphasis and unity are useful.

Balance refers to the distribution of differently 'weighted' elements on a page. **Optical weight** is essentially how eye-catching the element is:

- dark elements weigh more than light elements;
- coloured elements weigh more than greyscale elements;
- bright colours weigh more than pastel shades;
- large elements weigh more than small elements;
- elements far from the central vertical axis weigh more than elements close to the axis;
- irregularly shaped elements weigh more than regularly shaped ones;
- moving elements weigh more than static ones.

Symmetry (Figure 5.11) involves the distribution of equally weighted elements about a vertical axis down the middle of a layout and is very easy to use. For each element of a certain weight on one side of the axis, we place an element of equivalent weight in the same position on the other side of the axis. It results in very formal, conservative layouts, but can be dull. An asymmetrical layout distributes elements of different weights on opposite sides of the axis, but tries to maintain a balance – rather like a set of scales. A 'heavy' element on one side can be balanced by a couple of lighter elements on the other side. This can lead to an informal, exciting and dynamic layout, but it can also result in a layout that is hard to read and that detracts from the content. Asymmetrical layouts are harder to get right than symmetrical ones.

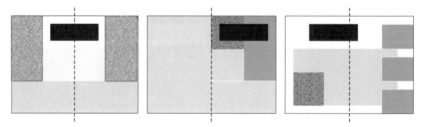

Figure 5.11 Symmetrical, unbalanced asymmetrical and balanced asymmetrical layouts

Weight is also an important factor in the **sequence** of a layout. The sequence is the order in which the user's eye is drawn from one element to another. In addition to the standard reading order (top to bottom, left to right), the weight of an element has a strong influence on the sequence, with 'heavier' elements catching the eye first.

The **proportion** of our layout, in terms of how the screen is divided into columns and rows, is an important aspect of our layout design. Even proportions (halves, quarters – Figure 5.12) are more formal than uneven ones (thirds, fifths). The most important informal proportion is the one-third to two-thirds proportion, which can be applied in a vertical and/or horizontal orientation (Figure 5.13). For example, we may have a layout that uses one-third of the screen for navigation and two-thirds for content, or one-third for text and two-thirds for images.

Figure 5.12 Half/half proportions: vertical, horizontal and combined

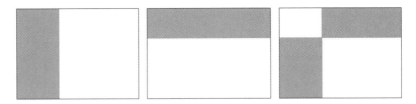

Figure 5.13 One-third/two-thirds proportions, vertical, horizontal and combined

Elements that overlap the boundary of a proportion can add excitement to a layout, but overuse can ruin the effect of the proportion.

We can use a **page grid** (Figure 5.14) to define our proportions. This involves dividing up the available screen space into a grid of rows and columns and using this grid to position our media elements (Figure 5.15). A grid system is useful for ensuring consistency, but can lead to layouts that are predictable and boring.

Figure 5.14 A five by three page grid

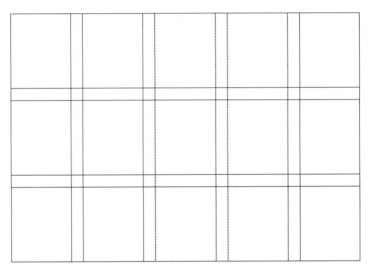

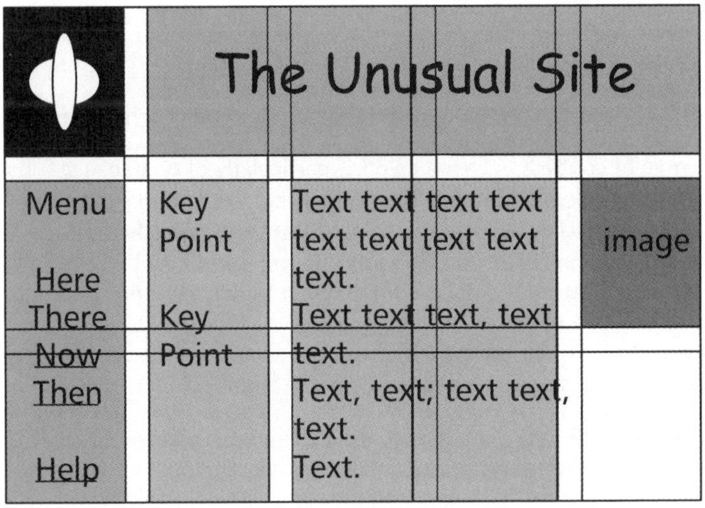

Figure 5.15 A layout based on a five by three page grid

Emphasis involves making one element in a layout the focus point. This can be difficult to achieve in a screen that mixes different multimedia elements and optical weight is an important factor. Techniques we can use to emphasise an element include:

- to isolate it from other elements using whitespace;
- to use colour to emphasise it;
- to place it in a dominant position in the middle of the screen;
- to use movement to draw attention to it.

Unity refers to the degree to which all the elements of the layout work together to present a consistent look and feel. We wouldn't want to use cartoon illustrations or silly sound effects with text on a serious subject. This may also apply to the application as whole, not just individual screens.

Colour is an important aspect of visual design. One of the things we need to understand about using colour in our design is **why** we are using colour. We may be using colour for a variety of different reasons:

- to enhance the aesthetic appearance of a screen;
- to draw the user's attention to a specific part of the screen;
- to emphasise important information;
- to identify different parts of the screen and its logical organisation;
- to group similar items together;
- to impart content information to the user;
- to indicate status (on/off, selected/not selected).

We also need to be aware that colours and colour combinations will make different impressions on our users in terms of their emotional impact:

- harmonious colour combinations can create a relaxed, calm impression;
- highly contrasting colour combinations can create an impression of excitement and dynamism;
- warm colours (reds, oranges, yellows) can create an impression of friendliness and liveliness;
- cool colours (blues, greens) can create an impression of efficiency and precision;
- neutral colours (greys, browns) can create an impression of sophistication and elegance;
- dark colour combinations can create an impression of enclosure or foreboding;
- light colour combinations can create an impression of freedom or space;
- colours have different meanings in different cultures, try to follow common colour meanings within the user's culture or workplace.

Other factors we need to consider when designing our colour scheme include:

- The degree of contrast between colours, particularly of text against a background.
- Don't overuse colour as this will overwhelm the user and make the application difficult to use. Pick a few key colours and use them consistently.
- Do not rely only on colour to distinguish things, users may be colour blind and colours will appear differently on different computer monitors, in different browsers or when printed.
- Make your colours and the way you use them suitable for your users and the application. For instance, children may prefer bright colours.

Many multimedia applications are aimed at inexperienced and casual users, our application must be easy to understand and use. One way we can approach this is by making our application look and behave like something the user is already familiar with – this is known as an **interface metaphor**.

For example, we may use the metaphor of a book, making the application look and behave like a book. We can use a background which looks like paper and divide the screen into two pages. We can make it behave like a book, perhaps we navigate by clicking a page-turning icon at the bottom corner of the pages. We might include an animation of a page turning as a transition. We could extend the behaviour to allow the user to include bookmarks.

The metaphor makes it easy for the user to get started. However, there are going to be things that you can do with a book that you can't do with the application and there will be things you can do with the application that you can't do with a book. As the user learns where the metaphor breaks down, they will gradually stop thinking of the application as being like a book and instead will learn the way the application works.

It can be difficult to find appropriate metaphors, we should always try to find a metaphor that is familiar to the users and which makes sense for the application.

Quick test

1. What makes multimedia screen layout design different to page layout design?
2. What are the five basic principles of page layout?
3. What features make one element more 'weighty' than another?

Section 5

Interactivity

In this section we briefly consider some of the ways that we might add interactivity to our multimedia application.

CRUCIAL CONCEPTS

Interactivity involves the user manipulating the content in some way. It can be very powerful and can set multimedia applications apart from traditional forms of media, such as books.

One of the powerful things we can incorporate into our multimedia application is **interactivity**. Rather than have our user passively viewing our content, we can give them the opportunity to interact, to do something with the content in a stimulating way.

CRUCIAL TIP

Interactivity is not the same as navigation. Navigation is simply moving through the content, interactivity is manipulating the content.

We can provide a range of interactivity, including:

- **Simulations** where the user can change the parameters of the simulation to see what the effect of the changes are.
- **Games** where the user controls characters or events.
- **Quizzes, tests and puzzles** where the user can enter text, or drag and drop elements.
- We may allow the user to **customise and personalise** the application by adding new content or new links, or by restructuring existing content.

It is not going to be appropriate to include interactivity on every screen of every multimedia application. There will be some applications for which interactivity is simply inappropriate.

We should be looking for opportunities to use interactivity to enhance the user experience. We also need to ensure that the interactivity we provide is suitable for both the users and the type of application. In an educational application aimed at young users we may include games and puzzles. An educational application aimed at adults may use simulations and tests.

Quick test

What is the difference between navigation and interactivity?

Section 6

End of chapter assessment

Multiple choice questions

1. A 'chunk' is –
   a) a paragraph of text
   b) a screenful of content
   c) a media element on a screen
   d) a coherent block of content.

2. A good structure is one which reflects –
   a) the developer's view of the content
   b) the user's view of the content
   c) structure inherent in the content
   d) the client's view of the content.

3. The two most common structures are –
   a) network
   b) sequential
   c) composite
   d) hierarchical.

4. Are these layout proportions formal or informal –
   a) halves
   b) thirds
   c) sevenths
   d) eighths.

5. Using an interface metaphor means –
   a) making the interface look and behave like a book
   b) making the interface look like a three-dimensional world
   c) making the interface look and behave like something the user is familiar with
   d) making the interface look like a VCR.

Multiple choice answers

1. d) is the right answer. A chunk may be a paragraph of text and it may be a screenful of content, but this is not always the case.

2. b) and c) are the right answers. In most cases the inherent structure and the user's view will be the same.

3. b) and d) are the correct answers. c) is also common, but is made up of sequences and hierarchies.

4. Formal, informal, informal, formal. Even proportions are formal.

5. c) is right. All the others are just examples of metaphors.

Questions

1. Explain the meaning of 'structure' in the context of multimedia applications. Illustrate your answer with examples of common structures.

2. Define 'navigation' and give examples of three navigation aids that might be used in a multimedia application.

3. Define the five principles of page layout, and explain what they mean for multimedia design.

4. Explain the concept of 'optical weight' and show, with examples, how the concept is used in designing symmetrical, unbalanced asymmetrical and balanced asymmetrical layouts.

5. Give examples of how interactivity can be used in multimedia applications.

Answers

1. We are being asked to *explain the meaning of 'structure'* and *illustrate our answer with examples of common structures*. Our answer should start by explaining what structure is – a navigable organisation of content. We need to explain that the raw content has been broken into chunks and that navigation refers to the user moving from chunk to chunk. The structure defines the routes through which navigation may occur. (If you imagine that the chunks are cities, then the structure is the road network between the cities.)

   We are asked to illustrate our answer with examples – if it makes sense within the context of a question, it is always useful to literally illustrate with a diagram. We should notice that we are being asked to illustrate *common* structures. We should definitely include sequences and hierarchies in our answer. We will sketch an example (see Figures 5.1 and 5.3), but also explain why we might want to use the structure. For hierarchies we want to discuss the issue of balancing depth and breadth. For sequences we could discuss branching paths (see Figure 5.2). We would probably want to include composite structures too.

2. We are being asked to *define 'navigation'* and to give *three examples of navigational aids*. We know that navigation is the process by which a user moves through the structure of an application. We can also explain that users will navigate for different reasons: finding out how it works, browsing, re-orientating, seeking information and returning to information.

   We might then list all of the navigational aids: links and buttons, search, backtracking, history list, bookmark list, site maps and guided tours. We would also give a very brief description of those that we aren't going to use as examples. This just help to show the lecturer that we know this topic well.

   We would then concentrate on our three examples in more detail. We should be careful to pick examples that give us something to say, perhaps they are an interesting contrast, or work well together. We would include a sketch if this helped explain the navigational aid. We would also give examples of when it might be appropriate to use them, maybe in certain types of application or for certain types of user. This shows that we don't just know what they are, we know about their strengths and weaknesses and can make judgements about when they are appropriate.

3. We are being asked to *define the five principles of page layout*, and *explain what they mean for multimedia design*. The five principles are: balance, sequence, proportion, emphasis and unity. We need to define each of these and relate them to multimedia. As well as relating them to multimedia, we would identify situations where multimedia offers new potential:

   - **Balance** – our answer will include the concept of optical weight and what features give a media element weight. We should note that in multimedia we can include motion as an extra feature that adds optical weight. We will also discuss the notion of symmetrical and asymmetrical layouts, how this relates to balance and how it influences the 'feel' of a layout.

   - **Sequence** – we will refer to the idea that the eye is drawn to elements. We can relate this to the issue of the user not being sure how to 'read' a multimedia screen.

   - **Proportion** – this applies quite directly in multimedia layout. We should discuss the different impression that even and uneven proportions can create. We can mention page grids as a tool to help us design a layout with set proportions.

   - **Emphasis** – we can refer back to optical weight and some of the other techniques we can use to emphasise an element.

   - **Unity** – we can talk about the consistent overall look and feel of an application. We should mention that the users and content will have an influence on the look and feel. We can also mention that consistency helps the user understand and remember the interface.

4. We are being asked to *explain 'optical weight'* and *show, with examples, how the concept is used in designing symmetrical, unbalanced asymmetrical and balanced asymmetrical layouts*. We can start by saying that optical weight is essentially a measure of how eye-catching a media element is. We would then list the features that contribute to optical weight.

   We then need to describe what symmetry and asymmetry are and distinguish between balanced and unbalanced asymmetry – remember this hinges on the idea of an imaginary vertical axis down the centre of the layout. We will illustrate these with sketches similar to those in Figure 5.11. We can also discuss the different impressions that the different layouts create and the fact that asymmetrical layouts are harder to do well.

5. We are being asked to *give examples of how interactivity can be used in multimedia applications*. First we should define interactivity, even though the question doesn't directly ask us to – interactivity involves the user manipulating the content. We should note that interactivity hasn't yet been exploited to its full potential in multimedia applications. Referring back to Chapter 1, Section 7, we could mention games as a good example of interactivity, but we need to be clear that this is only one possible use. Other possibilities include: simulations, quizzes, tests, puzzles and customisation. If we can think of real world examples of these, we should definitely include them – perhaps you are using some online learning material as part of your course. Don't get too distracted by explaining how good the latest game you bought was – keep it relevant.

   We should also mention that interactivity won't always be necessary and it should only be used to enhance the user experience, rather than just for the sake of it. We should also consider that the type and amount of interactivity will be influence by our users, their tasks, the content and so on.

Section 7

Further reading and research

Reading

Cloninger, C. (2001) *Fresh Styles for Web Designers*, New Riders.
Holzschlag, M. E. (2001) *Color for Websites*, RotoVision.
Wands, B. (2002) *Digital Creativity*, John Wiley & Sons.

Research

Keep a folder full of interesting designs you come across. These could be screen dumps of Web pages, pages from magazines, pamphlets or even packaging materials. Try to categorise them into general types. This then forms a useful reference source when you are working on your own designs. It can also be a good idea to carry round an instant camera with you in case you come across design inspiration – perhaps building interiors or clothes.

Chapter 6
Development techniques

Chapter summary

In this chapter we first look at a number of different informal design documents. We then look at prototypes, what they are and how we can use them during a development. Finally we look at different methods of evaluation.

Learning outcomes

After studying this chapter you should aim to achieve these targets by answering the questions at the end of the chapter. You should be able to:

> **Outcome 1: Identify the characteristics of the different informal design documents.**
> **Outcome 2: Recognise the role and use of prototypes with multimedia application development.**
> **Outcome 3: Appreciate the issues involved in designing, conducting and reporting an evaluation.**

How will you be assessed on this?

In an exam you may be asked to describe the different design documents and explain why they are useful. You might be asked to create examples of the different documents. Questions on prototypes may ask you to explain what they are and relate them to the iterative cycle. Questions on evaluation may ask you to describe the different techniques, or to select evaluation methods suited to a particular scenario.

In coursework that required you to build a multimedia application, you might be expected show your design process. This would take the form of the design documents that you have produced. It would also include a description of any prototypes you have produced or the prototypes themselves. You will often be asked to evaluate your designs or applications.

Section 1

Design documents

In this section we examine the different informal design documents that can be produced during the development of a multimedia application and in particular during the iterative cycle.

CRUCIAL CONCEPTS

We will produce a variety of different **design documents** during the development process. These are essential for communicating design ideas. **Personas and scenarios** help us focus on users and their tasks. **Structure charts** describe the organisation of content and **flowcharts** illustrate user navigation or interaction. **Storyboards** and **wireframes** are useful for designing screen layouts.

During a development we will use a number of different design notations (ways of expressing our design). Some of these notations will be quite technical, for instance entity-relationship diagrams for database design. While these technical notations are very precise, they are typically not good for communicating with users, so they are not appropriate for user-centred design.

What we require are design documents that express the important aspects of our design in a way that is easily understood by people without a computing background. As we are likely to produce a large number of these documents, it is important that they are cheap to produce.

We will start with fairly abstract descriptions of our application, such as the client's initial concept and the requirements identified during the requirements analysis. We will then consider our users and tasks in more detail. Based on this we can design the structure of the application and the navigation and interactivity. Finally we will design the look and feel of the application.

Personas and scenarios

Personas and scenarios describe our key users and how they will use the application. They are created during requirements analysis, but feed into the design phase. They can also be useful in prototyping and evaluation.

A **persona** is a description of an invented character that is representative of one of our key user groups (Figure 6.1). As our application will generally have more than one type of key user, we will have more than one persona. For each persona we will have:

- a name and photograph – this allows us to talk about them and relate to them as a real person;
- personal characteristics and background to flesh out the persona;
- a brief description of their characteristics which are relevant to the application we are developing;
- a list of their goals and attitudes when using the application;
- a list of factors which will influence the way they are able to use the application.

Personas are useful for getting us to think about the characteristics of our users, what motivates them and what they are interested in. The information in our personas is based on data gathered from our users, in interviews, questionnaires and focus groups.

Once we have defined our personas, we can write scenarios that describe the way a particular persona will use the site. We are likely to have several scenarios for each persona as a person may use an application for different reasons.

A **scenario** is a description of how a persona uses the application to achieve their goal. Sometimes these will be quite high level, whilst at other times we may write scenarios that describe each individual interaction the user carries out. In some cases we may include storyboards (Figure 6.7) to illustrate our scenarios. An example scenario is shown in Figure 6.2; there would also be a persona for Janet. There may also be other scenarios for Janet describing her other typical activities.

Both personas and scenarios can be as detailed or as high level as you like. They should also include whatever information is relevant to your design.

CRUCIAL TIP

Two basic terms for users that apply to many applications are 'new users' and 'frequent users'.

Jonathan
30 years old
Male
Single

Laboratory assistant earning £24K
Educated to degree level in chemistry

Typically reads a book a week, likes to follow particular authors, but is always looking for new authors who write similar types of book. Also interested in series and masterwork collections. Likes to read books which are recommended by friends with similar tastes. He has a large collection of books and sometimes finds it difficult to remember which ones he has.

Uses the internet most evenings, generally for checking email. Doesn't use it for long periods as modem is slow and access costs are high. Reluctant to use online shopping as he is concerned about security.

Wants to see new titles from favourite authors
Wants easy access to favourite authors
Wants to see titles from similar authors
Wants recommendations from people with similar interests
May wish to make recommendations
May wish to be able to record which books he already has
May wish to create 'wish-list'
Wants ordered books to arrive quickly
May wish to use offline payment methods
May be interested in opening an account
May like to have notification of new titles sent by email

Does not want to spend long browsing site
Speed of site will be important
Needs to be reassured about security and confidentiality

Site needs to provide convenience beyond that provided by a bookshop

Figure 6.1 Example persona for an online bookshop

1. Janet is a regular user of the site and has the URL stored in her bookmarks.
2. On arrival at the site Janet is presented with a list of new releases since her last visit, in her favourite categories of music.
3. She browses the list, marking some to be added to her 'wish-list'.
4. Janet spots a new release from her brother's favourite band and emails the details to him.
5. Janet has just had a pay rise, and decides to treat herself to a couple of new CDs so she reviews her 'wish-list' which now includes the latest releases which she has just added.
6. Browsing down she notices that some of the CDs are marked 'bought as gift for you' – she guesses that her brother has bought these for her birthday next week. Knowing that her brother likes the same music as she does, Janet leaves these CDs on her 'wish-list' in case her brother decides to keep them for himself. She can always remove the 'bought as gift for you' mark later.
7. She notices a CD on her 'wish-list' that she has been meaning to buy for a while, so she adds it to her shopping basket.
8. Another CD on the list catches her eye, she opens up the track list and plays a sample track. Deciding that she likes the sound of it, she adds it to her shopping basket.
9. Janet does this for several other CDs, then notices that the shopping basket total, which is continuously displayed on the screen, has reached £75. This is more than she wanted to spend because she also wants to treat herself and her fiancé to a meal to celebrate her pay rise.
10. She decides to review her shopping basket and reluctantly removes some of the CDs back to her 'wish-list', watching as the basket total is reduced to £50. She knows that the price displayed includes VAT and postage, so this is the actual amount that she will pay.
11. Janet's credit card details are already stored, so all she has to do is enter her password to verify the transaction. A confirmation message is displayed confirming her purchases. Janet prints this for her records, then leaves the site.

Figure 6.2 Example scenario for an online CD shop

Structure charts

Multimedia applications consist of chunks of content linked together into a navigable structure. A **structure chart** is a simple graphical representation of this structure, showing how content is organised. A structure chart consists of two basic elements, screens (or pages) indicated by boxes and links indicated by lines (Figure 6.3). A link between two screens shows that it is possible to navigate between them. Typically a link doesn't indicate a direction for navigation, but we can show this using arrows if necessary.

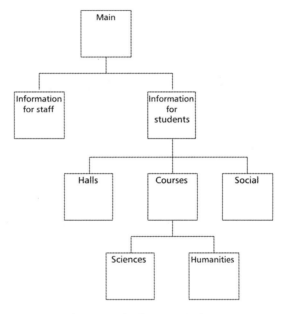

Figure 6.3 Simple structure chart

One difficulty with structure charts is that they can become overcomplicated if we try to include too much detail. Suppose that in the structure chart shown in Figure 6.3 the 'Humanities' screen has a direct link back to the 'Main' screen. We could show this by joining the 'Humanities' and 'Main' screens with a line. However if all the screens have a link back to the 'Main' screen and we show all these, the structure chart will become confusing. Instead we define a set of common links and identify these with a shortcut notation. We may define 'M' as the shortcut for a link to the 'Main' screen. We then include this shortcut on any screen that has a link to the 'Main' screen, instead of drawing the line. We can see an extended version of the structure chart in Figure 6.4. We have introduced a shortcut notation: M – link to Main, H – link to Help. It is important to include this information in a key on the structure chart. We have added a numbering system to the screens, e.g. S1.2.3. This allows us to refer to the relevant storyboards, but has also been designed to reflect the structure itself. For example, any storyboard whose number starts with S1.2 will be information for students. In practice you will need to adopt your own system of numbering for storyboards, structure charts, flowcharts and other design documents, so that you can cross-reference between them. The internal structure of the elements has been refined to include separate areas for references and shortcuts.

The element representing the screen 'Information for staff' has been modified to show that there are in fact several screens in this section, but they are not all shown. In this case we have included a reference number (SC02) to the structure chart which expands this section. We have also attached comments to the structure chart.

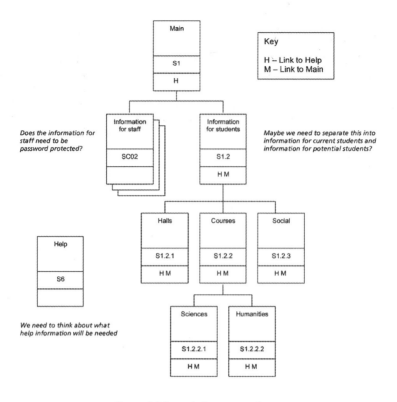

Figure 6.4 Extended structure chart

Flowcharts

Multimedia applications almost always involve user interaction and 'flow' or navigation between different parts of the application. **Flowcharts** are a simple graphical format which describes this interaction and the potential paths that the user may follow (Figure 6.5).

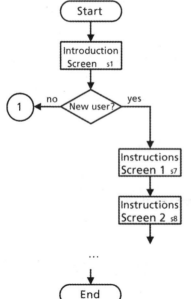

In order to relate the flowchart to the storyboards or wireframes, each screen element has a reference to the equivalent storyboard (e.g. s1).

Note the connector to another page. The connector on the other page will also be numbered 1.

The 'new user' decision is part of the 'Introduction Screen' screen – though it may be a pop-up window over the screen.

The flowchart does not specify how the 'new user' question is actually answered (e.g. it could be user interaction, or automatic), or how the flow from 'Instructions Screen 1' to 'Instructions Screen 2' is caused (e.g. it could be user interaction, or on an automatic timer), it just shows the flow. The storyboard for the screens would contain this information. If we wanted to distinguish between user interaction decisions and automatic decisions or timers, we could introduce a new flowchart element. It is important that we document any new elements and use them consistently.

Figure 6.5 Example flowchart

The difference between a flowchart and a structure chart is that the structure chart represents the static organisation of content and links, whilst a flowchart represents the potential dynamic movement of a user through that structure and interaction with the content. You should adapt and extend flowcharts to suit your working practices and the applications you are developing. However, there are some standard conventions for the elements of a flowchart (Figure 6.6):

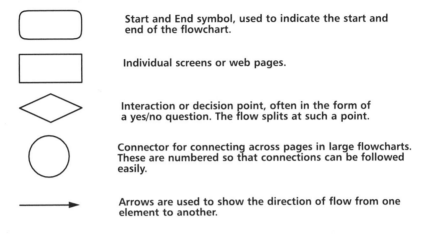

Start and End symbol, used to indicate the start and end of the flowchart.

Individual screens or web pages.

Interaction or decision point, often in the form of a yes/no question. The flow splits at such a point.

Connector for connecting across pages in large flowcharts. These are numbered so that connections can be followed easily.

Arrows are used to show the direction of flow from one element to another.

Figure 6.6 Standard flowchart elements

Storyboards

Storyboards are used to design the visual layout of screens or Web pages. Storyboards can be used to design both static screen layouts and dynamic elements, such as animations.

A **storyboard** is a rough sketch of a screen layout, or a sequence of sketches illustrating a dynamic element. This sketch is not necessarily well drawn, as it only needs to illustrate the concept of the layout. Sometimes we may produce better quality sketches, perhaps if we are intending to use them as part of a presentation to clients.

In addition to the sketch, there is a variety of supporting information about:

- colours;
- text content;
- sizes and types of font;
- script of any narration;
- audio;
- animation;
- video;
- interactivity;
- linking.

Further information can be included if appropriate. Much of this will be in written form, though it will often include the filenames of appropriate media elements.

Other information will include a reference number for the storyboard so that we can cross-reference between design notations and other administrative information, such as date of creation, version number and author (Figure 6.7).

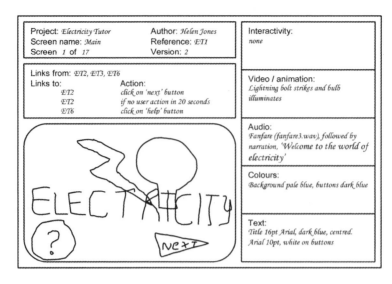

Figure 6.7 Example storyboard

In addition to paper-based storyboards, we may produce electronic storyboards, perhaps in Microsoft PowerPoint, Macromedia Director, plain HTML or a specialised multimedia project package. This has the advantage that we can include digital media. This can give a more accurate impression of what the design looks like.

Wireframes

Wireframes are similar to storyboards in that they are a mock-up of a screen layout (Figure 6.8). Whilst storyboards are mainly concerned with the aesthetics of the screen layout, **wireframes** focus on the organisation of content and navigation. Wireframes are likely to be used by an information architect rather than by the creative designers, though the creative designers may refer to the wireframes when they are designing the visual look and feel of the application.

Wireframes can be used to investigate a number of design issues with users, including:

- sequencing of screens;
- labelling of screens for orientation and navigation purposes;
- ordering of items on menus and menu labels;
- organisation of content on a screen;
- organisation of content into sections and subsections.

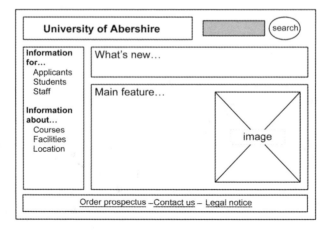

Figure 6.8 Example wireframe

Wireframes are often implemented as linked Web pages because this provides a functional structure that can be tested with users. Users will not be expected to produce or modify the wireframes, though the developer may make quick modifications in response to user comments during testing.

The design documents discussed here can be used at many stages of an application development, from generating and presenting the project proposal through to planning a redesign. They are not only useful for communicating with clients and users, they also provide a focus for the design team. On completion of the development, the documents form a vital part of the archive.

There are some drawbacks with these informal documents. The first is the lack of precision; it is possible for these informal documents to be misunderstood, so it is important for the project manager to check that people are consistent in the way they use them. A useful technique to avoid misunderstandings is to bring team members together around these documents for meetings. The second drawback is that of scalability. These documents are easy to produce for small applications, but do not always scale up well to larger applications. Larger application developments tend to rely more heavily on formal documents, though they often still use informal documents for communicating with clients and users.

--- CRUCIAL TIP ---

These design documents should be created *before* your implementation. Design documents produced after the implementation often look very false and don't explain the design process well, which may lead to lower marks for these elements.

Quick test

1. How are personas and scenarios related?

2. What is the difference between a structure chart and a flowchart?

3. What is the difference between a storyboard and a wireframe?

Section 2

Prototypes

In this section we examine prototypes, what we use them for, the different types and how we can produce them quickly and cheaply during the iterative cycle.

--- CRUCIAL CONCEPTS ---

A **prototype** is any kind of mock-up of the application that can be used to communicate design ideas and to evaluate them. During the **iterative cycle** we will create and evaluate many prototypes.

A **prototype** is a mock-up of the multimedia application being developed. This is used to communicate ideas and designs (both technical and creative) to the clients and users and between development team members. Most importantly, it is used to evaluate these ideas and designs.

A prototype may focus on one small aspect of the overall design, or it may mock-up the entire application. The scope of the prototype depends on the question we are trying to answer. The three common prototype scopes are full, horizontal and vertical prototypes (Figure 6.9). Horizontal prototypes are appropriate when testing the look and feel, vertical prototypes are appropriate when testing the functionality. One particularly useful variation of the vertical prototype is a scenario-based prototype, where we mock-up only the parts of the application and functionality required by one of our scenarios. This helps us focus on user tasks.

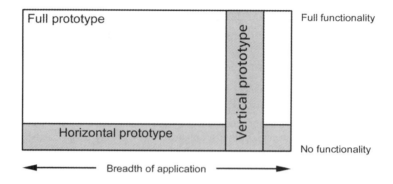

Figure 6.9 Full, horizontal and vertical prototypes

The iterative cycle will involve the development of a number of prototypes, many of which are going to be used to answer a question and will then be discarded. We therefore need to make our prototyping quick and cheap (**rapid prototyping**). This can be achieved in a number of ways:

- use paper prototypes, such as storyboards, instead of electronic prototypes;
- don't worry about the quality of your media elements;
- use fake media elements if the real elements are not available;
- use members of the development team to simulate functionality if it hasn't been implemented;
- don't worry about the efficiency or reliability of the implementation;
- use simplified algorithms that don't handle all cases;
- limit the scope of the prototype to that which is absolutely necessary.

When using these approaches we must make sure that the focus of the evaluation won't be compromised. For example, if we are evaluating the acceptability of the speed of response, it would give misleading results if we use simplified algorithms, or less efficient code. If we are presenting our prototype to the clients to evaluate the overall look and feel of the application, we *should* be concerned with the quality of the media elements.

The most common way prototypes are used within the development process is illustrated in Figure 6.10. Initial design ideas are mocked-up in a number of experimental prototypes. These are evaluated (ideally with users) and one is identified as the best. Good features from the other prototypes are also noted and included into a full prototype, now with higher production standards. This full prototype is then evolved into an alpha version through repeated redesign, refinement of the prototype and re-evaluation (the iterative cycle). It is likely that smaller horizontal or vertical prototypes focused on specific design issues will also be created during the evolution of the full prototype.

─────────────── CRUCIAL TIP ───────────────

All the design documents discussed in Section 1 are a form of prototype and can be used in an evaluation.

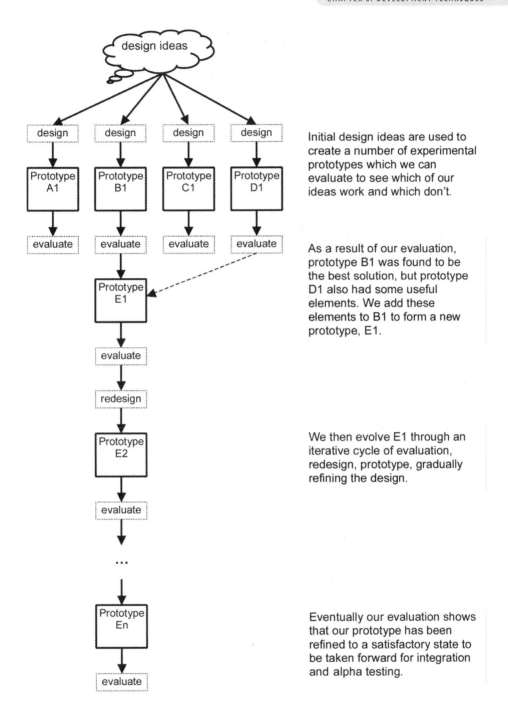

Initial design ideas are used to create a number of experimental prototypes which we can evaluate to see which of our ideas work and which don't.

As a result of our evaluation, prototype B1 was found to be the best solution, but prototype D1 also had some useful elements. We add these elements to B1 to form a new prototype, E1.

We then evolve E1 through an iterative cycle of evaluation, redesign, prototype, gradually refining the design.

Eventually our evaluation shows that our prototype has been refined to a satisfactory state to be taken forward for integration and alpha testing.

Figure 6.10 Evolution of prototype to alpha testing

Quick test

1. What is a prototype used for?

2. What are the differences between full, horizontal and vertical prototypes?

79

Section 3

Evaluation

In this section we examine some of the methods for evaluating prototypes and for gathering information at other stages of a development.

─────────────── CRUCIAL CONCEPTS ───────────────

Evaluation is the testing of design ideas, prototypes and applications. Ideally this evaluation is performed with users. Evaluation can take a variety of forms. **Observation** involves watching test subjects use the prototype. We can **gather users' opinions** through questionnaires and interviews. We may perform formal **experiments** under controlled conditions. We may observe the user in their working environment, this is known as **contextual enquiry**. In **predictive evaluation** we use interface experts to predict user problems. We can also gather information once an application is launched, through **feedback** and **log analysis**.

Evaluation is concerned with answering questions about a design, typically a design expressed in the form of a prototype. We may perform evaluations to answer a number of different questions at different stages in the development lifecycle:

- What does the user want?
- What tasks do users currently perform?
- In what order do users want to perform tasks?
- How do users perform tasks?
- Can users perform their tasks using this interface?
- Which design is faster to use?
- Which design results in fewest errors?
- Which design is the easiest to use at first encounter?
- Which design is the most memorable?
- Which design is the most enjoyable?

The two main approaches to evaluation are formative evaluation and summative evaluation. **Formative evaluation** is performed as part of the design process – the evaluation we perform in the iterative cycle is formative. **Summative evaluation** is the evaluation of a completed application. We may perform summative evaluation of an existing system before redesigning it, or of our competitors' applications before developing our own.

Evaluations can be classed as qualitative or quantitative. **Qualitative evaluations** focus on descriptive, subjective, non-numerical factors. We might be interested in which design the user finds more pleasing. **Quantitative evaluations** focus on things that can be measured and statistically analysed. We might be interested in which menu layout allows users to complete tasks the fastest.

An evaluation consumes a lot of resources – our time, the time of our test users, the cost of equipment and the cost of the facilities. It is important that we do not waste these resources through poor preparation. We should use an evaluation plan which lists the important factors relating to our evaluation, including:

- The goal of the evaluation – what question are we trying to answer?
- Where and when will the test take place and how long will it take?
- What computer system is needed for the evaluation?
- What initial state should the system be in at the start of the evaluation?
- Who are the test users going to be and how many are required?

- What tasks will each user be asked to perform?
- What data is going to be collected and how?
- What analysis will be conducted once the data has been collected?
- How will the analysis answer our evaluation question?

─────────────────── CRUCIAL TIP ───────────────────

Classmates and family members can be used as test users. However, you need to consider whether they are representative of your real user population. If they are not, your results may be flawed – you can still use them but you should discuss this weakness in your report.

When we are evaluating with test users we need to be aware of the **ethical implications**. Behaving in an ethical manner is an important part of professional practice. We can behave ethically by:

- Only using volunteers.
- Using a consent form and making sure that consent is informed (the test users know what they are agreeing to).
- Letting them know how long the evaluation is going to take.
- Ensuring that test users know they can quit at any point during the evaluation.
- Reassuring them that it is the design that is being evaluated, not them.
- Guaranteeing them that all results will be anonymous.
- Making sure they are comfortable during the evaluation, perhaps including a break in a long evaluation.
- Not wasting their time: be prepared, don't keep them waiting, keep the evaluation focused on the question.
- Not letting them struggle with a particular test task, if they are struggling then there is something wrong with the design (or the test task). Allow the user to move on to the next task before they become frustrated or disheartened.

The evaluation should be an enjoyable experience for the test users.

There are a number of different evaluation methods that can be used. Each method has advantages and disadvantages. Typically we will use a combination of methods to answer a question, either in the same evaluation or in different evaluations.

Observation involves watching the user performing tasks with the application and recording their performance in some way. The tasks may be the users' real tasks, or we may create test tasks. We can use a number of recording techniques:

- We can sit and watch the user and record significant events by hand, possibly guided by a checklist. This is useful if we are interested in something quite limited or specific. It is hard to record a wide variety of different events accurately.
- We can use video recording or screen capture software to capture the on-screen behaviour of the user. It is useful for recording **what** the user did. We can combine this with audio recording. We can also show the video to users after the interaction and get them to comment on **why** they did what they did (known as a post-event protocol).
- We can use audio recording to capture the users' comments. A think aloud protocol involves encouraging users to talk about their thoughts and decision-making process as they are using the application. Whilst this can give a useful insight into **why** the user did something, users can find it disruptive. It also gives no indication as to **what** they did.
- We can use software logging to record the users' interaction with the system. This is a text log of each on-screen event, such as clicking on a button, recorded against time. It provides a very accurate record of **what** the user did.

We should be aware that the test user's performance may be influenced by the observation and we should make it as unobtrusive as possible.

Gathering users' opinions involves allowing the test user to interact with the application and then asking them for their opinions. We might use a questionnaire or interview. We can use questionnaires to gather a variety of data:

- demographic information about the user (age, occupation, etc.);
- technical information about the user's computer or network;
- the number of times the user has used the application;
- the user's purpose in using the application;
- how the user found out about the application;
- which pages or screens the user accessed;
- whether the application was useful to the user;
- whether the user was satisfied with the experience of using the application.

A questionnaire may consist of closed questions where the user selects an answer from a set of alternatives and open questions where the user provides their own answer. Closed questions are easy to analyse, but restrict the user's responses. Open questions are harder to analyse because there is no restriction on the type of answer that may be given, on the other hand it allows for answers that you hadn't anticipated.

There is a lot of information on how to design questionnaires. Some general guidance is to:

- explain the purpose of the questionnaire to the user;
- only ask questions that will give you the answers you need;
- only ask questions that the user will be able to answer;
- only ask questions that the user is willing to answer;
- make the questionnaire quick to answer;
- place important questions at the beginning of the questionnaire;
- questions must be clear and unambiguous;
- include an 'any other comments' section – this can be useful for information you hadn't anticipated;
- thank the user for completing the questionnaire.

Interviews can be either structured, where there is a fixed set of questions, or semi-structured where general topics are used to guide the interview, but other topics can be pursued if they seem important. Semi-structured interviews rely more on the skill of the interviewer.

In formal **experimentation** the test user performs specific tasks under experimental conditions. The user's performance is accurately measured and the quantitative data gathered is analysed using statistical methods. Whilst an experiment can provide us with very accurate data, it may tell us little about how the system will perform in the real world.

Contextual inquiry involves observing the user in their real working environment. The users may be actively involved in collecting, analysing and interpreting the data. Methods might include observation, questionnaires, interviews, focus groups or user diaries. Contextual inquiry is particularly useful for obtaining requirements.

Predictive evaluation doesn't involve test users at all. Instead interface experts review the system, often against a set of guidelines, and predict the problems that users will encounter. The experts typically present their finding in a report that includes recommendations as to how problems can be solved. A criticism of predictive evaluation techniques is that they can falsely predict problems that real users will never have.

Once an application has been launched, we can conduct a summative evaluation by gathering feedback from real users who are using the application in the real world. **Feedback** could be in the form of an email, or via an online questionnaire. Another method is **log analysis** where we automatically keep a record of which users access which pages. This can be useful for building up a picture of real user behaviour, though it can be hard to pinpoint specific problems with the application.

Quick test

1. Is the analysis of a competitor's application a formative or summative evaluation?

2. What is the difference between an open question and a closed question?

Section 4

End of chapter assessment

Multiple choice questions

1. Which of the following design documents is best for focusing on users as real people?
   a) storyboards
   b) flowcharts
   c) personas
   d) structure charts
   e) scenarios
   f) wireframes.

2. Which of the following design documents is best for expressing the visual appearance of screens?
   a) storyboards
   b) flowcharts
   c) personas
   d) structure charts
   e) scenarios
   f) wireframes.

3. Which is the best way of making prototyping quick and cheap?
   a) use simplified algorithms
   b) use paper prototypes
   c) limit the scope of the prototype
   d) use fake media elements
   e) use lower quality media elements.

4. Which of the following evaluation methods does not involve users?
   a) contextual inquiry
   b) log analysis
   c) predictive evaluation
   d) experimentation.

Multiple choice answers

1. c) is the right answer, though you could also argue that e) scenarios also make us focus on users as real people.

2. a) is the right answer. If you answered f) wireframes, remember that these focus on the organisation and labelling of content on a screen, rather than the visual (aesthetic) appearance.

3. This is a trick question. Any of the answers could be right depending on the reasons we were constructing the prototype.

4. c) is the right answer.

Questions

1. Explain what personas and scenarios are and discuss why they are used in multimedia application development. Write an example persona and scenario for an online CD store.

2. Explain what structure charts and flowcharts are and discuss why we would use both in multimedia application development. Draw an example structure chart and flowchart.

3. As a project manager you are concerned that your prototyping will be too slow and expensive. Describe some approaches that can be adopted to avoid these problems.

4. You are planning a summative evaluation of an existing tourist information kiosk, prior to redesigning it. Outline the things you would wish to discover through your summative evaluation and indicate the evaluation methods you would use.

Answers

1. We are being asked to *explain what personas and scenarios are* and *discuss why they are used*. We are also asked to *write an example persona and scenario* for an online CD store application.

   We can start by setting the general context, pointing out that communication is important in multimedia developments and that we need simple design documents to explain our designs to users and to clients to get feedback. These documents also help communication within the development team. They will form an important part of the project archive.

   We would then move on to describe personas, what they are, what information goes into one and why they are useful. We would do the same for scenarios and stress the relationship between personas and scenarios – remember each persona may have several associated scenarios.

   In terms of writing examples, we need to use some common sense and a little imagination. We can use the example persona in Figure 6.1 as a template, making the actual detail appropriate to the application we have been given. We would try to think of a typical key user type. The example scenario in Figure 6.2 is appropriate to the application we have been given – however we would not try to memorise the actual scenario as we can draw on our own experience to come up with scenarios. It would make sense to write a scenario appropriate for the persona as this shows how they work together.

   Don't get too carried away with fanciful personas and scenarios, we are only trying to illustrate what they are, not provide complete polished design documents.

2. We are being asked to *explain what structure charts and flowcharts are* and *discuss why we would use both* in multimedia application development. We are also asked to *draw an example structure chart and flowchart*.

   As with Question 1, we can start by setting the general context, pointing out that communication is important in multimedia developments and that we need simple design documents to explain our designs to users and to clients to get feedback. These documents also help communication within the development team. They will form an important part of the project archive.

   We would then move on to describe structure charts, what they are, what information goes into one and why they are useful. We might briefly mention the relationship between structure and navigation. We would do the same for flowcharts and stress the difference between the two – structure charts represent the static organisation of content and links, whilst a flowchart represents the dynamic movement of a user through that structure and interactivity. We can talk about the dynamic movement of the user in terms of navigation, which ties in nicely with structure. The two diagrams are therefore complementary views of the design, we need to design and explain both the static and dynamic aspects of our application.

   In terms of drawing the examples, we haven't been given an application so we will need to invent one. Ideally we will choose an application that we can use for both the structure chart and the flow chart, this illustrates how they are used together. We do not need to provide large examples, so long as they show the key features of both diagrams. For the structure chart we could draw something similar to Figure 6.3, though we may wish to include some of the extra features shown in the extended chart in Figure 6.4. We need to explain what the different features are, this relates back to the earlier part of our answer. For the flowchart we would produce something similar to Figure 6.5, showing the use of the different elements in Figure 6.6.

3. Even though this initially sounds like a project management question, it isn't – it is a question about prototypes. We are being asked to *describe some approaches that will make our prototyping quick and cheap*. We should start by explaining why our prototypes need to be produced quickly and cheaply – relating this to the iterative cycle and the difficulties in knowing beforehand how many prototypes we will need to build. We should also introduce the concept of rapid prototyping.

   The approaches we can use are listed in Section 2. We can discuss full, horizontal and vertical prototypes as well.

   We need to mention that we should be careful in applying these approaches in case we compromise our evaluation, for example if we are presenting our prototype to the clients to evaluate the overall look and feel of the application, we should be concerned with the quality of the media elements and should probably avoid using fake media elements.

4. We are being asked to *outline the goals of our summative evaluation* and *indicate the evaluation methods we would use*. We have not been given much information about the project resources or about the purpose behind the redesign. We should start by making and stating our assumptions. We should only make assumptions that are reasonable.

   The actual content of this answer will vary quite a lot depending on the assumptions that we make and the goals we set for our evaluation. The fact that the application already exists gives us some clues, we can gather users' opinions about the existing system (questionnaire, interview, onscreen questionnaire), we can observe them using it (checklist, possibly video though this may be too intrusive) and we can keep logs of user interactions. Observation is probably going to be more appropriate than contextual inquiry because the users are only likely to be using the application for a short period of time (remember – it is an information kiosk). We could ask users to take part in an experiment, but we may learn more by observing real life use. We could use predictive evaluation, but as we have a ready source of real users with real tasks (and real problems) we may choose not to use it and perform more observations or opinion gathering instead.

Notice that we are discussing methods even though we are saying that we won't use them – this shows the lecturer that we are aware of the other methods and that we can make reasoned judgements about them.

Section 5

Further reading and research

Reading

Barnum, C.M. (2002) *Usability Testing and Research*, Longman Publishers.

Brinck, T., Gergle, D. and Wood, S.D. (2002*) Usability for the Web: Designing Web Sites that Work*, Morgan Kaufmann Publishers.

Rosenfeld, L. and Morville, P. (2002) *Information Architecture for the World Wide Web*, O'Reilly.

Wodtke, C. (2002) *Information Architecture: Blueprints for the Web*, New Riders.

Research

Look in books and on the Web to find examples of design documents (designers often have examples in their online portfolios). Compare these and identify any features that you think are particularly useful. Create your own templates in a drawing or word processing package. You can use these when designing your own multimedia applications.

Chapter 7
Text

Chapter summary

This chapter provides the theory and principles of text creation and manipulation. Text is the underpinning component of any multimedia application.

Learning outcomes

After studying this chapter you should aim to achieve these targets by answering the questions at the end of the chapter. You should be able to:

Outcome 1: Appreciate the use of text in multimedia.
Outcome 2: Explain the characteristics of text.
Outcome 3: Explain the principles of computer based text.
Outcome 4: Explain the process of creating fonts.

How will you be assessed on this?

In exams you could be asked to explain where and how text can be used to enhance the communication with the user; describe how text characters are defined. In coursework you could be asked to explain in what ways you have used text to help communicate with the user.

Section 1

Text in multimedia

In this section we explain the various ways in which text can be used effectively in multimedia applications.

Humans have been using sequences of symbols or text to communicate meaning for at least 6,000 years and today it is still the most powerful and efficient way of communicating ideas (provided you understand the symbols being used). Text is a sequence of symbols where each symbol has meaning but the arrangement of symbols can convey even more meaning. Text is used in multimedia applications to communicate key concepts and as part of the navigation. As with any piece of text choosing the right combination of words can dramatically affect its fidelity and impact in a multimedia application. When using text in multimedia one must strike a balance between the quantity of text and the amount of space on the screen. You should not use long pieces of text in multimedia applications – this is better off being printed. Text in multimedia needs to be engaging and succinct and should be drafted, redrafted and then edited to ensure it is right.

It is difficult to imagine designing the structure and navigation of a multimedia application without using text somewhere. Text is used for buttons, instructions, tool bars and supplementary information. When using text within the structure and navigation it is even more important that the words are succinct and convey the right meaning – there are subtle differences between saying 'back' and 'previous'. The space available may also mean significant editing of a passage of text to make it fit. Particular care needs to be taken with the words when applications are for an international audience or will be translated into different languages.

───── CRUCIAL CONCEPTS ─────

Text is the most powerful and efficient means of communicating ideas. Text that is used in navigation design must be succinct and care must be taken over the choice of words.

───── CRUCIAL TIP ─────

You should be able to explain why text is important and how it is used in multimedia applications.

Quick test

What is important about text in multimedia applications?

Section 2

Terminology

In this section you will learn about the terms used to describe the characteristics of text.

Text used in multimedia applications share many of the same characteristics as printed text which have been evolving since the first printing presses in the fifteenth century. A text's **typeface** defines its 'character' i.e. the features and similarities between each letter which make letters of the same typeface seem like they belong with each other. Figure 7.1 shows the same word presented in four different typefaces: (a) is Times Roman, (b) is Arial (c) is Jokerman and (d) is Viner Hand.

(a)   (b)   (c)   (d)

Figure 7.1 Different typefaces

It is possible to have variations within a typeface, e.g. change of size, bold or italic characters. When you choose a particular variation of a typeface, e.g. 12 point, bold it is called a **font**. Typefaces therefore represent families of fonts. Figure 7.2 shows four fonts within the Arial typeface. The terms typeface and font have become confused and are generally interchangeable when used in the context of computing. For the rest of this chapter we will use the term font.

(a)   (b)   (c)   (d)

Figure 7.2 Different fonts within the Arial typeface

Characters in a typeface are described by a number of attributes as shown in figure 7.3.

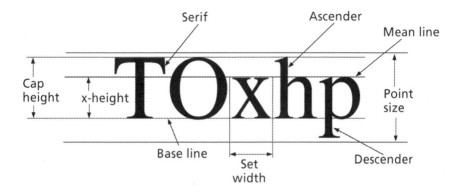

Figure 7.3 Attributes of a typeface

Font sizes are measured in 'points' which are equal to 0.0139''. The size of a font is measured from just above the top of any capital letters to just below the bottom of the descender on letters like g or p. The font size is not a precise description of its height, two fonts of the same point size may have variations in their **x-height** which is defined as the height of their lower case x. Some typefaces/fonts are said to be **serif,** which means each letter has a curl-like decoration on end points to help guide the eye along the text. Other typefaces/fonts on the other hand do not have serifs and are referred to as **sans-serif** (sans is the French word for 'without').

The gap between two lines of text is referred to as **leading** (pronounced as 'ledding').The leading is generally controlled by software in computer based fonts. **Tracking** refers to the standard distance between each character, the higher the tracking the more spaced out a word appears. The distance between particular pairs of characters can be altered automatically to produce more natural looking words. This process is referred as **kerning**. Figure 7.4 shows the difference between an 'A' and a 'w' with and without kerning using Adobe Photoshop.

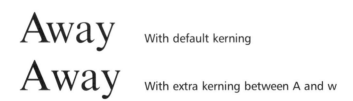

With default kerning

With extra kerning between A and w

Figure 7.4 Kerning between 'A' and 'w'.

CRUCIAL CONCEPTS

Typeface: A set of symbols, i.e. the alphabet, that share common features giving the letters a common style.

Font: A subset of a typeface of a particular point size and style, e.g. Helvetica 12 point, bold.

Point size: Unit of measurement of size of font equal to 0.0139 inches.

Leading: The distances between two lines of text.

Tracking: The standard distance between characters in a font.

Kerning: The adjustment made between the spacing of particular character pairs to make the text look more natural.

Quick test

What is the difference between a typeface and a font?

Section 3

Computer based text

Computers can make the development and presentation of text easier and more interesting. Computers can provide you with many useful tools for manipulating and displaying text.

In computers which pre-dated the Apple Macintosh, text on the screen was very basic and could normally only be displayed in one basic font which was not the same as that which was printed. The introduction of the Macintosh enabled people to see on the screen what was actually printed (what you see is what you get – WYSIWYG). The Macintosh mapped each character code to a specific bitmap held in a table and stored in memory. The problem with bitmapped fonts was the need to have a specific bitmap for each character for every size and variation of font, hence placing great demand on computer memory. In 1985 Macintosh adapted Adobe's vector based technique for displaying and printing fonts in **Postscript**. Since Postscript is vector based, fonts could be scaled and styled with much greater speed and ease. Any size of character could be displayed without requiring a new bitmap. Postscript fonts are classed either as type 1, 2 or type 3 (there are other types). Type 1 fonts are mainly used in computer based applications, type 2 in Adobe Acrobat files and type 3 fonts are used primarily by the print industry. Apple introduced a new system for defining fonts called **TrueType** which were faster to display than Postscript.

Both Postscript and TrueType support a technique called hinting. When a vector based font is scaled up or down, sometimes the resulting character does not look right, e.g. the cross bar in a capital 'A' will look too thin. By adding hints to the details of the font when fonts are scaled the hints ensure small changes are made to ensure characters remain looking good. A particular font might have thousands of hints added to make it legible.

Today, Microsoft Windows supports bitmapped, Postscript and TrueType fonts and likewise for Macintosh System 7 machines. In Windows based machines fonts are managed from the control panel using the interface shown in Figure 7.5.

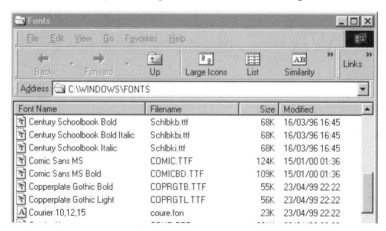

Figure 7.5 Managing fonts with Microsoft Windows

Despite all the advantages of vector based fonts, bitmapped fonts are still used where small characters are required like the system font. This is because the algorithms used in vector based fonts have problems adequately describing small fonts. The designers of bitmapped fonts can make subtle handmade changes to each character bitmap to improve its readability. Hence the 'Small fonts' system font on Windows machines is bitmapped. Whether a font is bitmapped or not, it will appear 'jagged' on the screen as shown in Figure 7.6(a) unless anti-aliasing techniques are applied as in Figure 7.6(b) (see Chapter 8 for an explanation of anti-aliasing).

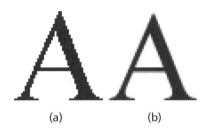

(a)   (b)

Figure 7.6 (a) Text without anti-aliasing (b) text with anti-aliasing

Care must be taken when designing an application that requires particular fonts. If any of the fonts that you have used in your application are not available to the end user and you have not embedded the fonts with the application, the destination machine will replace it with something else. This is equally true of applications designed to run on both Macintosh and Windows machines, where slight differences between the same font like Courier can make text appear very different and spoil screen layouts.

Until the early 90s characters were encoded in memory in a system called **ASCII** (American Standard Code for Information Interchange). ASCII represents each character as a value between 0 and 256, i.e. a single byte. ASCII only uses 7 bits (that means 128 different characters) which leaves space to encode another 128 characters. These extra 128 characters are called the extended character set and are usually filled with the standard characters of the American National Standards Institute (ANSI) which includes many often used symbols and characters. Apple introduced a new standard in the early 90s called **Unicode** which uses 2 bytes to represent up to 65,000 different characters. Unicode enables computers to display languages that use different or extra symbols to the British alphabet, like Russian Cyrillic.

Including text in Web documents presents its own problems. The same Web documents may be viewed in different browsers, on different machines running different operating systems and with different installed fonts. To control the presentation of Web pages designers can try a number of techniques. Designers can build their Web pages with functions that examine what browser and operating system is viewing the page. When the routines know these things they can dynamically make changes to the Web page like adjusting the width of tables. Another trick is to automatically download any special fonts used in the page or use a free program from Microsoft called Web Embedding Fonts Tool (WEFT). Another technique is to prepare text that uses unusual fonts as bitmaps. However, the simplest technique is to use only the standard fonts supported by the browser like Arial or Times Roman.

The most common tool for manipulating text is a word processor and most, like Microsoft Word, have built-in wizards to create interesting looking text, as shown in Figure 7.7. However the problem with this technique is transferring the text into a multimedia or Web page because of the proprietary nature of the image format.

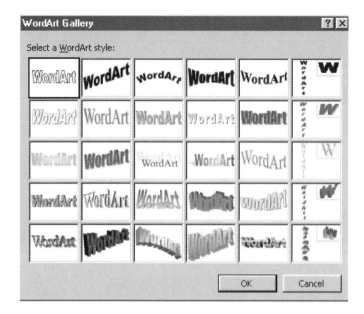

Figure 7.7 WordArt in Microsoft Word

One of the most effective ways of creating engaging text is to work with it as a bitmap using an image editing tool like Adobe Photoshop or Jasc Paint Shop Pro, or a vector based image editing tool like Adobe Illustrator. These tools allow designers to transform rather dull text into something very eye catching instead. Figure 7.8 shows how the simple text 'Study Schedule' used as a heading in an educational web site has been changed from rather plain text to something much more interesting and informative using Adobe Photoshop. All the text was created in the font Bank Gothic, the first letter of the foreground text is 24 point, and the rest 22 point with a drop shadow effect added. The background text is of a larger point size with an opacity of only 5% so the foreground text appears through. An image of a schedule has also been added to the image to convey extra meaning and interest.

Figure 7.8 The words 'Study Schedule' created as a heading in Adobe Photoshop

Computers can significantly enhance the presentation of text by animating it. Animation can be used to make headings, buttons or hyperlinks more noticeable, pleasing and sometimes more meaningful. In the animated GIF example in Figure 7.9 below the meaning of the text is enhanced by the text 'flying' from right to left across the image's width.

Figure 7.9 Example of animated text

CRUCIAL CONCEPTS

Postscript: A vector based technique for displaying and printing fonts developed by Adobe.

TrueType: A vector based technique for displaying and printing fonts developed by a consortium led by Apple.

Anti-aliasing: A technique for displaying characters on screen without a jagged effect.

ASCII: A standard for defining characters on screen.

Unicode: A newer standard for defining screen characters that provides for up to 65,000 characters.

Web based text: Developers must be aware of the limitations of browsers and the complexities of ensuring that text will appear as intended.

Animated text: Animating text can make it more engaging and help communicate the message/information.

Quick test

What is the problem with bitmapped fonts?

Section 4

Font editing tools

There are a number of tools available to edit existing typefaces or design entirely new typefaces from scratch. Perhaps the most common font design tool is Macromedia Fontographer. Fontographer enables designers to edit or create fonts from scratch. Figure 7.10 shows Fontographer being used to construct a new font called 'oddity' and Figure 7.11 shows the letter 'r' of 'oddity' being constructed. Font designers often begin creating fonts by sketching each letter either by hand or using a pressure sensitive stylus to vary the weight of the line strokes in the character. Once they have a good impression of what each letter will look like, it can be imported into Fontographer as a bitmap as shown by the grey outline in Figure 7.11. The designer can then trace around the imported bitmap with the vector outline of the character as shown in Figure 7.11. The next step is to add the hints to help computers display the typeface in difference sizes. Fontographer will add hints automatically, however most font designers prefer to do this themselves. Once each character has been created the new typeface can be output as either TrueType or Postscript.

Figure 7.10 Macromedia Fontographer being used to construct a new font called oddity

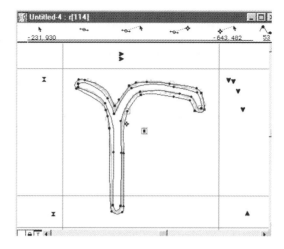

Figure 7.11 Macromedia Fontographer being used to construct the lower case
letter 'r' for the new font 'oddity'

CRUCIAL CONCEPTS

Font editing tools: These are tools that are used to edit or create new fonts. The most popular is
Macromedia Fontographer.

Quick test

Can you describe the process of creating a new font?

Section 5

End of chapter assessment

Multiple choice questions

1. Which of the following is an attribute of a font?
   a) serif
   b) Postscript
   c) paragraph
   d) bitmap.

2. Which one of the following is not an attribute of a font?
   a) kern
   b) tracking
   c) tracing
   d) baseline.

3. Which statement about computer based fonts is true?
   a) Bitmapped fonts are always preferred over vector based fonts.
   b) The advantage of bitmapped fonts is their scalability.
   c) Vector based fonts are the best for displaying small fonts on a computer screen.
   d) TrueType is a vector based font format.

4. Which statement about fonts and typefaces is correct?
   a) A typeface is a subset of a font.
   b) Typefaces and fonts are the same.
   c) Fonts are a subset of a typeface.
   d) A typeface is defined as a specific variation of a font.

5. Which statement is true?
   a) Type 3 fonts are generally used for computer based applications.
   b) Bitmapped fonts were developed to overcome some of the problems of vector based fonts.
   c) Anti-aliasing causes characters to appear jagged.
   d) Purposely designed bitmapped fonts are used to display small fonts.

6. Which statement is correct?
   a) ASCII uses 3 bytes to represent characters.
   b) ASCII can represent up to 65,000 characters.
   c) Unicode was developed to enable international character sets to be represented.
   d) Unicode uses a single bit to represent up to 127 characters.

7. Which statement about displaying text in a Web browser is true?
   a) Browsers support an extensive range of fonts.
   b) It is not possible to download fonts to a browser.
   c) Text displayed on different browsers and computers will look the same.
   d) Text in an unusual font should be prepared as a bitmap.

8. Which statement about creating and editing fonts is true?
   a) Fonts are created in word processors.
   b) Font designers often trace around a bitmapped graphic.
   c) Hints are used to help designers draw their fonts.
   d) Font designers generally start a new font by defining the hints.

Multiple choice answers

1. a)
2. c)
3. d)
4. c) is correct although in modern computing the terms font and typeface have become interchangeable
5. d)
6. c)
7. d)
8. b)

Questions

1. Explain why text is important in multimedia/Web applications.

2. What factors about text need to be taken into account when designing a multimedia/Web application?

3. Explain with the aid of a diagram the difference between the x-height of a font and its size in points.

4. Explain the difference between a bitmapped font and a vector font.

5. Describe the process of how a new font is typically created.

Answers

1. The points which need to be made in your answer are:
   - Text is the most powerful and efficient way of communicating ideas.
   - Text can be more succinct than other forms of media.
   - Text supplements the meaning of on-screen objects like navigation buttons.

2. The points which need to be made are:
   - Different browsers and different versions of browser support different ranges of fonts, therefore a limited range of fonts should be used for the bulk of text in a Web page.
   - Web pages can include code that checks to see what the type and version of browser is and adjust content accordingly.
   - Unusual fonts can be prepared as bitmaps.
   - There are tools available like Microsoft WEFT for embedding specific fonts.

3. You need to draw a diagram like that shown in Figure 7.3 showing the x-height, which is a good measure of the size of characters excluding ascenders and descenders. The size of font is measured in points equivalent to 0.0139 inches, but are not a true indication of the height of any characters but the height between the highest character and the lowest.

4. In a bitmapped font each individual character is represented by a bitmap for each point size and style of character. So, for example, a separate bitmap needs to be constructed for 'e', '**e**', 'e', 'e', '**e**', etc. for each point size required in the font and so on for every character in the font. In a vector based font like Postscript or TrueType a mathematical vector representation of each character needs to be constructed, but only once. Each point size and style of character can be generated from the one mathematical representation. Vector based fonts are therefore more flexible than bitmapped based fonts. However vector based fonts render poorly at point sizes below 10 points, so bitmapped fonts are specially constructed for small sizes, as is the case of system fonts on Windows based computers.

5. A designer usually starts to create a new font by sketching a few of the characters either on paper or using a tool like Adobe Illustrator or Photoshop. Once the designer has a clear idea of the nature and character of the new font they can start constructing the font using tools like Macromedia Fontographer. Most designers will take each character at a time and produce a bitmapped representation of it. The bitmapped representation of it is pasted into the font editing tool and the designer traces around the bitmap outline with a vector. Once designers are satisfied that the vector outline is a good representation of the new character they add 'hints' to the outline to help computers display the character in different sizes and styles. When designers have worked their way through each character they export the new font to either TrueType or Postscript.

Section 6

Further reading

Craig, J. (1999) *Basic Typography – A Design Manual*. Watson-Guptill.
Bringhurst, R. (1997) *The Elements of Typographic Style*. Hartley and Marks.

Chapter 8
Images

Chapter summary

This chapter provides the theory and principles of image construction. Images are likely to be a key component of any multimedia application. Studying this chapter will help you understand the difference between bitmapped and vector graphics, the principles of image compression and colour representation and how to create and manipulate images.

Learning outcomes

After studying this chapter you should aim to achieve these targets by answering the questions at the end of the chapter. You should be able to:

> **Outcome 1: Compare vector and bitmapped graphics.**
> **Outcome 2: Explain the principles of colour representation.**
> **Outcome 2: Explain the principles of image compression.**
> **Outcome 3: Explain the process of image creation and manipulation.**

How will you be assessed on this?

In coursework you should be able to explain what tools you used and why. In exams you could be asked to outline the general characteristics expected of image editing tools and describe the process of creating a bitmapped image.

In an exam you will be asked to explain the principles behind each type of graphic and the differences between them. In coursework you would be expected to explain your reasons for using a particular type of graphic or a combination of types, and what kind of treatment you gave each graphic, and be able to compare and contrast vector and bitmapped graphics.

Section 1

Vector and bitmapped graphics

In this section we outline the principles behind vector and bitmapped graphics and the reasons for the use of both methods of image representation.

Images are an important part of how we communicate with each other and, over time, human society has developed a sophisticated visual language to create and understand them. We can create digital images using a variety of methods. We can use a scanner to convert images from books or photographs into digital representations. We can use a digital still camera or even a digital video camera as sources for digital images. The other way of creating digital images is to use image-editing software like Adobe Photoshop or Adobe Illustrator in which case the image is in a digital format from the start. Images are displayed on monitors as a finite array of dots or picture – elements (**pixels**), where each pixel can display a range of colours. There are two main underlying approaches to creating the array of dots – vector graphics and bitmapped graphics (sometimes referred to as pixmapped).

Vector graphics represent the array of dots on the monitor that make up an image using a coordinate system similar to that used in coordinate geometry in mathematics, as shown in Figure 8.1. Each point is defined by a pair of values, so point A in Figure 8.1 is (1, 1) and point B is (5, 5). Shapes are defined by the key coordinates of their geometric representation plus an indicator of their shape, for example a simple black line on a white background can be represented by two coordinates as shown in Figure 8.1. Without the shape indicator all we would have are two dots on the screen. When a vector graphic is displayed, the display software converts the two coordinates of the line into an array of pixels. The display software does this by working out whether to display each pixel in the image as white or black as shown in Figure 8.1. The single line graphic can be stored in a file with just the two coordinates – (1,1), (5, 5), an indicator that it is a line, its thickness, style and its colour. All basic shapes like circles, ellipses, triangles, can be constructed using this technique and more complex shapes can be made from combining the basic shapes plus other instructions.

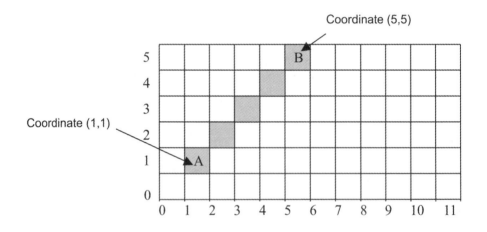

Figure 8.1 Coordinate system used to display a single black line

Bitmapped or pixmapped graphics represent the image by recording the colour of every individual pixel in the array. The image of the line in Figure 8.1 would therefore need to be stored as 72 values (12 columns by six rows).

CRUCIAL CONCEPTS

A **pixel** (picture element) is a single point in an array of points that constitute the image when it is displayed on a monitor.

Vector graphics represent graphics using a coordinate system to define the key points of a shape plus an indicator of the shape and then the display software works out how to display the intermediate points as pixels.

Bitmapped graphics represent graphics by listing the colour values of every pixel in an image.

Vector and bitmapped graphics have advantages and disadvantages and serve different purposes.

The advantages of vector graphics are:

- easily scalable without losing resolution;
- easy to select and manipulate elements of an image;
- generally less storage required.

The disadvantages of vector graphics are:

- complex images take longer for the computer to draw;
- no good for photorealistic images.

The advantages of bitmapped graphics are:

- good for photorealistic images.

The disadvantages of bitmapped graphics are:

- generally requires more storage than equivalent vector graphic;
- not easy to scale;
- not easy to select and manipulate elements of an image.

CRUCIAL TIP

You should be able to discuss the advantages and disadvantages of vector and bitmapped graphics

---

Quick test
What are the advantages of vector based graphics?

Section 2

Vector graphics

In this section we explain how more complex vector graphics are created, the principles of 3D graphics and discuss the problems of converting a vector graphic into a bitmapped graphic. The tools required to create vector graphics are also explained. The concept of anti-aliasing is introduced.

In Section 1 we explained how a simple line graphic can be stored as a pair of coordinates and some indicator that it is a line. Circles, ellipses and rectangles can all be represented as a pair of coordinates plus an indicator of its shape as shown in Figure 8.2.

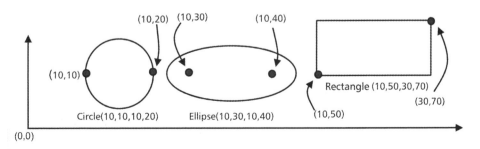

Figure 8.2 Creating basic shapes with vector graphics

More complex shapes like a rectangle with rounded corners require more information but the principle remains the same. **Polylines** are simply a set of coordinates mapping out a series of connected straight lines as shown in Figure 8.3.

Figure 8.3 A polyline

Curves require a particular geometric entity called a **Bézier** curve. A Bézier curve is defined by four coordinates, two coordinates indicating the beginning and end of the curve and two coordinates that control the curvature as shown in Figure 8.4. More complex curves are made up of a series of joined Bézier curves.

Figure 8.4 A Bézier curve

Vector graphics also allow you to change the style of a line from solid to various types of dots and dashes and its weight or thickness from heavy (6pt) through to light (¼pt). Polylines and Bézier curves can be joined together to form complex geometries for the image we wish to create (see Figure 8.5 (a)). These complex geometries are referred to as **paths**. Paths themselves are not visible on the screen but are the basis of what will become visible. Paths can be considered to be construction lines using a very light pencil which we then trace over with a thicker pen. Only when we apply a **stroke** (see Figure 8.5 (b)) to the path, giving it thickness, colour and style, does it become visible. When a polyline or curve forms a closed **path**, i.e. the end of the curve meets the beginning, one can fill the interior of the shape with a pattern or colour. In this case the path is referred to as a **fill** and simply serves as the outline of the shape (Figure 8.5 (c)). One could however choose to have the closed path filled and have the path visible in a different colour or style (Figure 8.5 (d)).

Figure 8.5 (a) Closed path (b) stroked path (c) filled path (d) path filled and stroked

A collection of vector graphics can be grouped together to form a symbol or library item. **Symbols** can be used again and again. For example, one could create a symbol of a house consisting of a few rectangles for the doors and windows and a triangle for the roof. If another house is required an instance of the house symbol can be placed on to the graphic without redrawing the whole house.

— CRUCIAL CONCEPT —

A **path** is the outline of curve or line in a vector graphic but is not visible until a stroke or fill is applied.

Quick test

Does a 'path' have any width?

Section 3

Bitmapped graphics

In this section we cover the principles of bitmapped graphics in more depth. We present the concepts of resolution and anti-aliasing.

In the first section of this chapter we explained that bitmapped images are represented by an array of pixels where each pixel represents a single dot in the image. **Resolution** is a measure of how finely the details of an image are represented. The measurement of monitor resolution is different from the measurement of image resolution. Monitor resolution is measured by the size of each screen dot (typically 0.26mm per dot or 97 dots per inch). The number of pixels per unit length, on the other hand, measures image resolution, usually in inches. Unfortunately there is not a simple correspondence between image and monitor resolution. On low resolution monitors each screen dot might equate to several image pixels whereas on high resolution monitors a single image pixel might be represented by several screen dots. Image formats like GIF and JPEG store the number of pixels per inch so that the image can be displayed or printed at the right size.

If the straight line shown in Figure 8.6 (a) was to be displayed on screen in its current state it would look jagged because it has to be represented by discrete pixels. This problem is illustrated in Figure 8.6(b): should pixel 'a' be black or white? The degree to which each pixel is included within the line will vary depending on how the line bisects it. The solution to this problem is to use **anti-aliasing** that renders each pixel along the line a different shade depending on how much of it is included within the line as shown in Figure 8.6 (c). When the anti-aliased line is displayed the human eye is fooled and sees a sharp edge rather than the mix of shades of grey along the line.

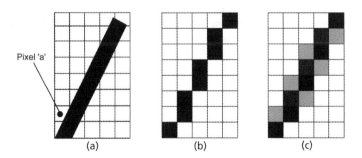

Figure 8.6 (a) Original line overlaid on a pixel array, (b) line represented without anti-aliasing (c) line represented with anti-aliasing using several shades of grey

---
CRUCIAL CONCEPTS

Image resolution is the number of pixels per unit length; **screen resolution** is the size of each screen dot. **Anti-aliasing** causes each pixel that falls along a straight line or boundary of an image to be painted a varying shade depending upon how much of it is included within the line/boundary. Anti-aliasing prevents straight lines looking jagged.

Quick test

What is the advantage of anti-aliasing?

Section 4

Colour

In this section we will explain how colour is represented in an image. This is important to understand because you will need to be able to balance the quality of an image with its size. Sometimes you will need to work with images from different sources that use different methods for representing colour.

The colour of an object is the result of certain wavelengths of electromagnetic radiation being absorbed by that object when light falls upon it. The eye receives the remaining wavelengths of electromagnetic radiation reflected off the object. When the light enters the eye it falls onto the retina where special cells called cones and rods are stimulated and transmit corresponding signals to the brain. The brain interprets the signals coming from the retina, so our sense of vision is therefore subjective. There are three types of cone, each stimulated by different wavelengths of light corresponding approximately to red, green and blue. We perceive different colours by the addition of different strengths of signal of red, green and blue coming from the cone cells.

Screen colour is created in a similar way to the cone cells of the eye by adding varying intensities of the colour component to each pixel and is referred to as **additive colour**. Black is created by the absence of any colour component and white is created by the maximum intensity of the colour components. Orange, for instance, is created by the addition of red and green with no blue. Printed colour on the other hand is created by taking colour away and is referred to as **subtractive colour**. White is created by the absence of colour (just the white paper) and black is created by the addition of the maximum values of the colour components. Subtracting different amounts of the three colour components creates all the other colours.

There are several models for representing the colour in an image. The most common of these is the Red, Green and Blue or RGB model, where the colour of each pixel is made up of values for each of the three colours. Other commonly used colour models are:

- **HSB** – **H**ue (colour), **S**aturation (intensity of colour) and **B**rightness (amount of black and white mixed with colour).
- **HSL** – Same as above only it refers to Brightness as **L**ightness.
- **L*a*b** – **L**uminance is the brightness of the colour (from white to black); '**a**' defines a colour range between green and red and '**b**' defines a colour between blue and yellow.
- **CMYK** – Example of a subtractive colour model used in printing where **C**yan, **Ma**genta, **Y**ellow and Blac**k** are used to produce the colour separations used in the printing process.

Whatever colour model is used, the colour of each pixel needs to be stored in computer memory. The amount of storage reserved for each pixel is referred to as its **bit depth** or **colour depth**. The amount of computer memory set aside for each pixel can vary from 1 bit per pixel to 24 bits or 3 bytes per pixel. Clearly with one bit per pixel we can only represent two colours. If we use 8 bits or 1 byte per pixel and the RGB colour model, we can use two sets of 3 bits to represent two of the colour components and the remaining 2 bits for the third colour component. 8 bits gives us a total of 256 combinations of values or colours. If we represent each pixel by 3 bytes (24 bits) we can use a whole byte for each colour component so we can represent up to 16,777,216 unique colours. Grey scale images (i.e. shades of black and white only) normally use either 8 or 16 bits per pixel. Unfortunately the more bits per pixel we use, the larger the image becomes, so we must ensure that an image only uses as many colours (i.e. bits per pixel) as is necessary to faithfully reproduce the image on the screen. Colour values are usually referred to using the hexadecimal notation for the red, green and blue components as shown in Figure 8.7.

	Red	Green	Blue	In full
Black	FF	FF	FF	#FFFFFF
White	00	00	00	#000000
Light grey	CC	CC	CC	#CCCCCC
Yellow	FF	FF	00	#FFFF00

Figure 8.7 Hexadecimal notation for colour values

The uncompressed size of an image file can be calculated using the following formula:

Size of file in bytes = (width in pixels × height in pixels × bit depth)/8

So for example an image which is 100 by 200 pixels with a 24 bit colour depth will be:

$(100 \times 200 \times 24)/8 = 60,000$ bytes

In another example an image which is also 100 by 200 pixels but only 4 bit colour depth will be:

$(100 \times 200 \times 4)/8 = 10,000$ bytes

One simple way the size of a file can be reduced is to utilise **colour lookup tables** (Macintosh term) or **Palettes** (PC term). Few images with a colour depth greater than 8 bits per pixel will use all the colours possible for that colour depth. So it makes sense to limit the number of bits per pixel to only cover the number of colours actually used. To do this we use a lookup table as shown in Figure 8.8. Assuming the bitmap in Figure 8.8 (a) has a colour depth of 24 bits then each pixel will require 3 bytes. However by using a lookup table as shown in Figure 8.8 (b) each pixel only needs to store the position of the colour it uses from the table. The image in Figure 8.8 only uses four colours so the lookup table only needs to store four values. Each pixel now only needs to be able to refer to one of four positions in the lookup table and that only requires 2 bits per pixel. So instead of using 3 bytes per pixel we only need 2 bits per pixel. The only problem with this approach is that the display software must now find the colours to use from the lookup table which takes fractionally longer than without a lookup table. A 24 bit image of say 200 by 300 pixels takes 200 x 300 x 3 =180,000 bytes to store. If the image only uses four colours we can store them in a lookup table, and then we only need to use 200 x 300 x 2 bits=120,000 bits or 15,000 bytes plus the lookup table 4 x 3 bytes=12 bytes – a total of 15,012 bytes to store the image. The use of a palette is usually referred to as indexed colour and the maximum size of palettes is 256 colours.

The other reason for using palettes is that many monitors, display adapters and Web browsers are limited to 256 colours which means that the software must map images of more than 256 colours to palettes of 256 colours. When display software attempts to do this it must make compromises between the original colours and the palette colours. The process for doing this is called **dithering** which attempts to recreate the colours not found in the palette. Dithering works by finding the closest match from the palette colours and then adjusting the surrounding pixels slightly to fool the eye into seeing the desired colour. Adobe Photoshop allows you to select dithering for images to be included in Web pages.

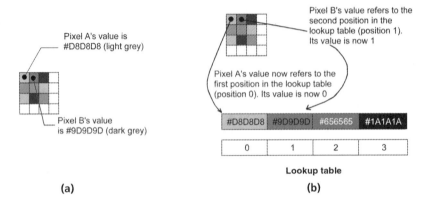

Figure 8.8 (a) is the normal way of storing a bitmap; (b) is the same bitmap utilising a lookup table

---

CRUCIAL CONCEPTS

Colour model refers to the way we represent the colour of each pixel. The most common model is **RGB** (Red, Green and Blue) which represents colours by specifying the intensity of red, green and blue for any given colour. Other models include **HSB** (Hue, Saturation and Brightness), **HSL** (the same except brightness is referred to as **Lightness**) **L*a*b*** (Luminosity, **a** green-red mix and **b** blue-yellow mix).

CRUCIAL TIP

You should be able to explain how bit depth affects the quality of image and file size.

Quick test

How can colour look tables reduce the file size of an image?

Section 5

Compression

Once an image has been created it needs to be included in a Web page or multimedia application. Although computers and networks are much more powerful and offer greater bandwidth than ever before, they still take time to load and display images. So ensuring images are kept as small as possible remains an important factor in image creation. Compression refers to techniques designed for reducing the size of an image file. Clearly when an image is to be displayed it must be decompressed.

The simplest compression technique called **run length encoding** (RLE) which works by counting runs of identical pixels instead of each pixel value. Consider the image in Figure 8.9 which is stored as an array of 30 values. As you can see we could represent this image simply as '14,5B,10,7F,8,00' which adds up to 6 bytes. RLE compression only works well where there are areas of the image of the same colour. When the RLE encoded image is to be displayed the software needs to regenerate the array of pixels in the image in a process called decompression. If the decompression process takes too long the user will become dissatisfied. So it is important to strike a balance between a small, heavily compressed image which takes time to decompress and display or a larger, less compressed one which will display more quickly but will take longer to transfer over a network or copy.

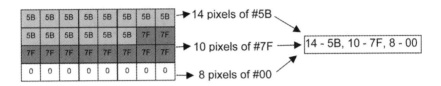

Figure 8.9 Run length encoding applied to a simple bitmap

Compression techniques fall into two distinct categories, **lossy compression,** which results in pixel information being discarded irretrievably and **lossless compression** which does not. Lossy techniques work on the basis of discarding information, which can be reconstructed with sufficient fidelity to fool the human eye. An image decompressed after lossy compression has been applied will not be identical to the original, uncompressed image. In comparison an image decompressed after lossless compression will always be identical to the original image. The advantage of lossy compression is that greater degrees of compression are possible compared to lossless compression. However a balance is needed between degradation in the quality of the image and greater degrees of compression. Ultimately, it is a matter of finding the degree of compression that affects the perceived quality of the image least. It is important, when working with image formats that utilise lossy compression, to keep a copy of the uncompressed origin, since successive applications of lossy compression will result in deterioration in the quality of the image. Many image formats use a mixture of several compression techniques one after another.

Huffman codes are sometimes used in lossless compression algorithms. These work by ranking the colours used in an image according to the frequency with which they occur. Then the shortest code (1 bit) is used to represent the most frequent colour and longer codes are used to represent the less frequent colours. More commonly used these days are algorithms based on 'dictionaries'. Dictionaries work by looking for repeating binary patterns in the image data and then ranking the patterns according to their frequency and length. The longest most frequent patterns are given the shortest codes. Lempel Ziv Welch (LZW) is the most well known example of a dictionary based compression algorithm and used in the GIF image format described below.

─── CRUCIAL CONCEPT ───

Compression is the application of techniques to reduce the size of an image prior to its inclusion in a multimedia or Web application.

─── CRUCIAL TIP ───

You should know why compression techniques are applied to an image.

Quick test

What is the disadvantage of lossless compression?

Section 6

File formats

The material covered in the previous sections becomes very relevant when considering what file formats to use for images. In this section we will look at how factors such as colour, compression and image characteristics affect the choice of file format.

There are many image file formats so we will only consider those most commonly used for vector and bitmapped graphics. You need to be aware that image editing tools should be capable of reading and converting between different formats. The most common vector graphic file format is PostScript developed by Adobe in the mid 1980s. The **PostScript** format is used extensively when printing to laser printers and is the basis of the Adobe Acrobat Portable Document Format (**PDF**) used in many Web-based documents. PostScript is a vector language for defining paths, shapes and fills and has been extended to include bitmaps and hyperlinks. Figure 8.10 shows a simple PostScript file for drawing an unfilled rectangle.

```
/cm {28 nul} def      % convert cm->points (1/28 cm)
newpath               % start a path
1 cm 1 cm moveto      % a cm in from the lower left
2 cm 1 cm lineto      % bottom side
2 cm 2 cm lineto      % right side
1 cm 2 cm lineto      % top side
closepath             % automatically add left side to close path
stroke                % draw the box on the paper
showpage              % eject the page
```

Figure 8.10 Simple PostScript file for drawing a filled rectangle

Usually tools like Adobe Illustrator are used for generating PostScript and it is unlikely you would create an image by writing PostScript code. If a PostScript image is to be incorporated in other documents it is converted into Encapsulated PostScript (**EPS**) format which includes a declaration of the overall dimensions of the image. The World Wide Web Consortium's Scaleable Vector Graphics (SVG) initiative is a simplified version of PostScript for optimising transmission of images over the internet.

There are three key file formats for bitmapped images used in Web and multimedia applications, the **Graphics Interchange Format (GIF)**, the **Joint Photograph Experts Group (JPEG) File Interchange Format (JFIF)** usually referred to as 'jpeg' or 'jpg' and the **Portal Network Group (PNG) format**. Some bitmapped image formats support **transparency** where particular pixels are designated as transparent. Transparent pixels are replaced by whatever colour lies immediately 'underneath' them on the screen. Applying transparency to an image enables non-rectangular images to be created, as shown in Figure 8.11 where the white pixels allow the background colour to show through. Another common file attribute is called **interlacing** and enables images transmitted over the Web to be displayed in a rough form prior to the whole image being downloaded. Interlacing works changing the order in which pixels are sent to the browser; instead of sending each row in turn, every second or fourth row is sent. The browser can then display these rows before the rest of the file is downloaded.

Figure 8.12 (a) shows an interlaced GIF image partially downloaded and 8.12 (b) shows the completely downloaded file.

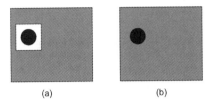

(a)   (b)

Figure 8.11 (a) image without transparency and (b) with transparency

(a)   (b)

Figure 8.12 (a) GIF image with transparency partially downloaded (b) image fully downloaded

Compuserve originally developed the GIF format as a common format for transferring images between different computer platforms. The GIF format utilises the lossless LZW compression algorithm and supports a maximum of 256 colours (8 bit colour depth). The limitation of 256 colours is not generally an issue unless the image has areas of subtly changing colours where 8 bit colour can cause contours to appear. The GIF format supports transparency and interlacing. The JPEG format supports 24 bit colour and utilises a powerful but lossy compression algorithm to give better compression ratios. In tools like Adobe Photoshop altering the quality of a JPEG image corresponds to changing the degree of compression, i.e. reducing the quality corresponds to increasing the degree of compression. Hence the final stage in producing a JPEG image involves adjusting the degree of compression to obtain the best compromise between file size and image quality. The JPEG format doesn't support transparency but does support interlacing (called progressive JPEG). The JPEG format works best on photo-realistic images with areas of subtly changing tones. JPEG should not be used on images of 1 bit colour depth or with clearly defined boundaries like lines and edges where it will cause some blurring as shown in Figure 8.13. The GIF format, on the other hand, works well with images that have clearly bounded areas of solid colour like cartoons. The PNG format was developed in response to the Unisys Company patenting the LZW compression algorithm used in GIF images. PNG uses a different lossless compression algorithm which is not patented, or restricted to 256 colours but does support transparency and interlacing. The PNG developers argue that it can be used in place of JPEG or GIF. The major Web browsers and multimedia authoring tools like Macromedia Director support the PNG format.

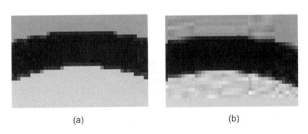

(a)   (b)

Figure 8.13 (a) 4 bit image saved as GIF and (b) saved as JPEG

CRUCIAL CONCEPTS

Graphics Interchange Format (GIF) utilises the LZW lossless compression algorithm and supports 8 bit colour depth and transparency. GIF is best suited to images that have clearly defined areas of solid colour and clear lines/edges like cartoons.

Joint Photographic Experts Group (JPEG) File Interchange Format (JFIF) utilises a lossy compression algorithm, supports 24 bit colour depth but not transparency. The JPEG format is best suited to photorealistic images with subtly changing tones.

CRUCIAL TIP

You should at least be able to compare GIF with JPEG file formats.

Quick test

When should you use the GIF file format?

Section 7

Tools

In this section we will be considering what characteristics image editing tools should possess. It is only when you start using these tools that a lot of the ideas covered in previous sections find their practical usage. You should know what basic functionality can be expected from an image editing tool.

There are tools specially designed to create and edit vector images like Adobe Illustrator and Coral Draw and there are specialist tools for creating and editing bitmapped images like Adobe PhotoShop and Jasc Paint Shop Pro. Most of these tools have some support for both vector and bitmapped graphics in the same file. As noted above, editing and manipulating vector graphics is much easier than bitmapped graphics because each element is explicitly represented in the file but selecting and manipulating elements of a bitmapped requires special techniques. The ability to resample/resize is not a straightforward process with bitmaps; the software must use special algorithms to determine how the pattern of pixels in the unaltered image is best represented in the altered image. For instance, doubling the size of a simple black line would make the line look grainy since each pixel in the original image is now represented by 4 pixels (this is not a problem with vector graphics) as shown in Figure 8.14. To select elements of a bitmapped image requires sophisticated **selection tools** that can identify the boundaries between areas of pixels. Some tools like Photoshop and Paint Shop Pro also allow elements of the image to be stored on separate **layers** making it easier to isolate and edit individual elements. For instance the text in an image can be stored on its own layer, so that it can be moved and edited independently of the rest of the image. The application of masks is another technique for isolating parts of the image for editing or omission from editing.

Figure 8.14 (a) Original line and (b) line increased in size by 5

Table 1 summarises the key characteristics that bitmapped image editing software should possess.

• file type conversion • direct input from scanner and other devices • sophisticated selection tools – lasso, magic wand • multiple windows to view several images simultaneously • ability to resample/resize images • adjust image brightness, contrast and colour balance • support image transformations – rotate, skew, distort and perspective	• multiple undo and restore capabilities • ability to blur, sharpen, lighten, darken, retouch, smudge • anti-aliasing support • capability to vary colour depth • layer support • filters for special effects e.g. distort, blur, stylise, render • drawing tools for basic shapes and fills and strokes • good masking features • create and edit colour lookup tables

Table 1 Characteristics of image editing tools

CRUCIAL CONCEPTS

Selection tools gives users the ability to select various parts of a bitmapped image. Selection tools use sophisticated algorithms to help identify the pattern of pixels that the user is trying to select.
Layers enable elements of the image to be kept separate from each other so that they can be edited without affecting the rest of the image.

Quick test

What is the advantage of the layers function in a typical bitmap editing tool?

Section 8

End of chapter assessment

Multiple choice questions

1. Vector graphics represent images by –
   a) an array of pixel values
   b) a set of coordinates with associated shape indicators
   c) an array of coordinates
   d) a coordinate system of shapes
   e) a set of pixel shapes.

2. Which option is the most precise definition of image resolution?
   a) the size of the image
   b) the total number of pixels in the image
   c) the dimensions of the image in pixels
   d) the number of pixels per unit length
   e) the physical size of each pixel.

3. Which of the following is not an advantage of vector graphics?
   a) able to represent photorealistic images
   b) easily scaleable
   c) easy to select elements of the image
   d) easy to transform image elements
   e) generally small file sizes for simple images.

4. Anti-aliasing is best described as –
   a) a pattern of pixels
   b) a technique for displaying photorealistic images
   c) a technique for displaying text
   d) a method for representing straight edges in a vector graphic
   e) a method for representing straight edges in a bitmapped graphic.

5. The most precise definition of colour depth is –
   a) the size of each pixel
   b) the maximum number of colours each pixel can display
   c) the number of bits available to display each pixel
   d) the number of colours used in an image
   e) the maximum number of colours used in an image.

6. Colour lookup tables are used to –
   a) reduce the number of colours used in an image
   b) reduce the size of each pixel
   c) identify how many colours are used in an image
   d) reduce the size of the image
   e) match the number of colours used in the image to the number of colours supported by the monitor.

7. Lossy compression is best described as a technique for –
   a) decreasing the colour depth
   b) encoding identical pixels
   c) encoding images for transferring over networks
   d) encoding images for minimum size
   e) reducing the size of photorealistic images.

8. Postscript file is best described as a format for –
   a) encoding bitmapped images
   b) encoding vector graphics
   c) sending information to printers
   d) representing Adobe Photoshop images
   e) representing Adobe Illustrator images.

9. The JPEG format is best suited to –
   a) vector graphics
   b) images with clear boundaries and solid colours
   c) 8 bit colour depth bitmapped graphics
   d) photorealistic images
   e) grey scale images.

10. Which of the following is not a typical characteristic of an image editing tool?
    a) support for layers
    b) sophisticated drawing tools
    c) sophisticated selection tools
    d) application of filters for special effects
    e) multiple windows.

Multiple choice answers

1. b) is the best answer but d) is partially right.
2. d) is the best answer e) refers to screen resolution.
3. a) is the correct answer.
4. e) is the best answer.
5. b) and c) are both correct.
6. The best answer is e) however lookup tables often result in d) reducing the size of an image and b) the size of each pixel.
7. e) is the best answer.
8. b) is the best answer but e) is partially correct.
9. d) is the correct answer.
10. b) is the correct answer.

Questions

1. What are the issues related to creating a bitmapped image for display in a Web browser?
2. Compare and contrast the use of vector and bitmapped graphics.
3. Calculate the size in bytes of an uncompressed image 300 by 400 pixels with a bit depth of 4 bits per pixel.
4. Explain how colour lookup tables work and how they can help to reduce the size of an image file.
5. Explain the differences between lossy and lossless compression.
6. Describe the process of bitmapped image creation.

Answers

1. Browsers only support GIF, JPEG and PNG formats. GIF is better for cartoon-like images whereas JPEG is better for photorealistic images; PNG can be used for either and is copyright free. Since browsers only support 8 bit colour you need to decide whether to enable image dithering so that its colours can be matched to that of the browser. You also need to decide whether to enable image transparency so that an image's transparency-colour displays the background colour of the Web page. You also need to decide whether to select progressive-JPEG or GIF with interlacing so that images begin displaying before being completely downloaded.

2. The advantages of vector graphics are: easily scaleable without losing resolution; easy to select and manipulate elements of an image; and generally less storage required. The disadvantages of vector graphics are: complex images take longer for the computer to draw; and no good for photorealistic images. The advantages of bitmapped graphics are that they are good for photorealistic images. The disadvantages of bitmapped graphics are: generally require more storage than equivalent vector graphics; not easy to scale; not easy to select and manipulate elements of an image.

3. Applying the formula for calculation a bitmapped image size:

   300 x 400 x 4/8 = 60,000bytes

4. Instead of storing its colour value, each pixel stores a pointer to an entry in a lookup table attached to the image. The entry in the table is the actual colour to be used for that pixel. Since lookup tables never have more than 256 entries, no pixel needs to be more than 1 byte long to be able to reference any one of the colour values contained in the lookup table. The advantage of this approach is that images of 16 or 24 bits per pixel colour depth can be reduced to 8 or less bits per pixel.

5. Lossy compression uses algorithms which result in images being reduced in size but where the process discards information irretrievably so that the uncompressed image is never identical to the origin. Lossless compression, on the other hand, does not discard any information so that the uncompressed image is identical to the original. Lossy compression usually results in much higher compression ratios than lossless compression. If there is no perceptible difference between the original and the uncompressed image, lossy compression is preferred. The JPEG format uses a lossy compression algorithm whereas the GIF format uses a lossless one.

6. Bitmapped images can originate from a number of sources – a digital camera or video, scanned pictures or from clip art libraries. Bitmapped images can also be created completely from scratch using an image editing tool. Whatever the origins of a bitmap it can be modified, edited and enhanced using bitmap editing tool like Adobe Photoshop. Bitmap editing tools enable users to combine images from different sources, modify aspects of the image like its colour, apply filters, effects and transformations. Once the image has been completed it can be output in the appropriate format for the application, e.g. GIF for Web pages, TIFF for desktop publishing.

Section 9

Further reading

Baxes, G. (1994) *Digital Image Processing: Principles and Applications*. John Wiley & Sons Inc.

Foley, J., van Dam, A., Feiner, S., and Hughes, J. (1995) *Computer Graphics, reissued 2nd Edition*, Addison Wesley.

Chapter 9
Animation

Chapter summary

This chapter provides the theory and principles of animation. Animation ensures users remain engaged with applications and can dramatically improve the communication of the message.

Learning outcomes

After studying this chapter you should aim to achieve these targets by answering the questions at end of the chapter. You should be able to:

> **Outcome 1: Evaluate the benefit of applying animation techniques in different situations.**
> **Outcome 2: Choose the right animation technique.**
> **Outcome 3: Apply the principles of animation to animation creation.**
> **Outcome 4: Determine which tools to use to create an animation.**
> **Outcome 5: Describe the process of 3D animation.**

How will you be assessed on this?

In an exam you could be asked to explain the purpose of animations in multimedia applications and apply the basic animation techniques to a given scenario. In course work you would be expected to explain how and why you have animated some elements of the application.

Section 1

Animation in multimedia

In this section we explain why animation is used in multimedia and Web applications.

Animation is most commonly associated with cartoons where characters are animated to create stories. However, any computer-based representation which includes pre-designed movement can be considered to be an animation – for example, icons. Just as static images can significantly improve the communication of a text message so animation can improve the communication of a message in a static image.

Animation can improve the **appeal** of an idea and **engage** the viewer, for example a logo for a building company could show a building growing over a few seconds or sequence through a series of images of all the company's services. Advertisements on the Web need to attract attention quickly when they are competing with many other advertisements, an engaging animation helps attract anyone browsing that page to a particular advertisement.

Animating a static image of a diagram can help to explain or better **illustrate** the principles encapsulated in the diagram. For example, a static image of the insides of a computer can be animated to show data moving around between the various parts of a computer (CPU, memory, printer etc.) during the execution of an instruction. Figure 9.1(a) shows a static illustration of the marketing communications process (Schramm, W. (Ed), *Communications in Modern Society*, 1948). Figure 9.1(b) shows a frame from an animated version where the 'message' is scrambled as it moves through the medium, at the same time the arrows move to illustrate the process.

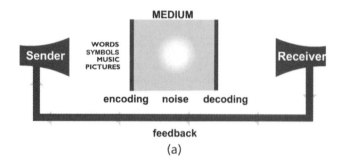

(a)

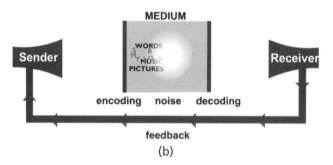

(b)

Figure 9.1 (a) A static illustration of the marketing communications process and (b) a still frame from an animation of the same illustration with the arrows moving along the feedback path and the 'SYMBOLS' becoming jumbled as they move through the medium.

───── CRUCIAL CONCEPTS ─────

Appeal: animations can make a concept like an advertisement more attractive.
Engage: animations can help keep the users' attention.
Illustrate: animations can help to explain concepts more clearly to the viewer.

Quick test

How can the use of animation help in the interpretation of a diagram?

Basics of animation

In this section we explain some of the fundamental techniques of animation.

Eadweard Muybridge's invention of the zoetrope showed how the eye could be deceived into seeing movement simply by showing a series of slightly different static images quickly in succession. Figure 9.2 shows a series of static images that form part of animation of a cartoon character walking.

- We call each static image in an animation a **frame** in exactly the same way they are called frames in digital video (see Chapter 11).
- We can change the size of the animation by changing the size of the frame. The **frame size** is defined by its height and width in pixels. In Web pages a typical animated banner advert is 120 by 60 pixels, television size animations are 640 by 480 pixels.
- The number of frames shown per second is called the **frame rate**. The higher the frame rate the smoother the appearance of the animation and animations need a frame rate of at least 10 frames per second to be convincing. Clearly the higher the frame rate and larger the frame size the larger the file size, which may not be important if the animation is going to be delivered on a CD-ROM but is important if it is going to be delivered over the Web.
- The concept of **colour depth** is introduced in Chapter 8 and is the same concept used in animations. The greater the colour depth the larger the animation file size. Colour palettes are used to reduce the size of files but maintain the number of colours used in an animation, see Chapter 8 Section 4 for an explanation of colour palettes.

Figure 9.2 Cartoon character walking

So far we have been referring to **frame by frame animation**, however the arrival of fast and powerful computers has enabled animations to be generated in real-time. **Real-time animation** means that instead of creating every single frame of the animation, the animator creates the important frames and the computer generates the rest at play time.

The advantage of frame by frame animation is the amount of control the animator has over the final animation. The disadvantage from the multimedia point of view is the size of the files and the time taken to create the animation. The main advantage of real-time animation is the relatively small file sizes generated.

CRUCIAL CONCEPTS

Frame by frame animation: the traditional approach to animation where each frame has to be individually created.
Real-time animation: the animator creates the important frames and the computer generates the frames in between. When the animation is displayed the computer again generates the frames in between.

CRUCIAL TIP

You should be able to explain each concept with reference to a simple illustration showing three or four frames.

Quick test

What is the difference between real-time and frame by frame animation?

Section 3

Basic animation techniques

This section looks at the basic techniques of animation which have evolved from the classic cel animation techniques

The techniques of computer based animation are essentially the same as the cel animation techniques invented in 1914 by Earl Hurd and developed by Walt Disney in the 1930s. The term cel animation comes from the use of sheets of transparent celluloid film to draw each **frame** of a sequence of animated action. The animators would start by drawing the frames for the beginning and end points of a fragment of action which were called **key frames**. A good example would be someone tripping over, the first key frame would illustrate the beginning of the trip and the last key frame would show the person stumbling and perhaps there would be another key frame of an intermediate point. Once the key frames have been draw the in-between frames can be drawn onto other sheets of celluloid in a process called **tweening.** The animation can be checked by flipping through all the frames laid on top of each other in 'play' order. The overlaying of all the celluloid frames on each other, and showing a slightly different moment in the animation, is often called **onion skinning**.

In repetitive animation sequences, like someone walking, it is only necessary to create the animation of one complete step and then copy and repeat it as required. The process of copying and repeating a repetitive animation sequence is called **cycling.** In situations where time and resources are scarce, animations are often created in a limited way. Instead of animating every little subtlety of an animation only the critical ones are animated. For example, when cartoon characters smiles, their mouths turns up at the corners, their eyes wrinkle and their cheeks move upwards. In a **limited animation** version perhaps only the mouth turning up at the corners is animated. The advantage of limited animation is the increased speed with which animations can be created and reduced file sizes, the disadvantage is the loss of a natural look to the animation.

Creating an animation

Animators plan out their animations using storyboards as described in Chapter 6. Storyboards are used by an animation team to consider the direction of the whole animation. Notes can be appended to a storyboard item to give extra information – like the sound requirements, which animator is responsible, etc. Figure 9.3 shows a sequence of storyboards to illustrate the bungy jumper with information about what sound is required.

Figure 9.3 Storyboard of man jumping off cliff

--- CRUCIAL CONCEPTS ---

Key frames are the beginning and end frames of a piece of action in an animation.
Tweening are the frames between key frames that complete the animation between key frames. Tweened frames can either be generated automatically or be drawn manually depending on the nature of the animation.

Quick test

Whare are the differences between key and tweened frames in an animation?

Section 4

Principles of 2D animation

We have explained the basic mechanics of creating an animation. However, in order to create effective animations you need to understand the principles that have to be applied to make animations convincing.

During the 1920s and 30s the Walt Disney studios developed a set of principles to help animators produce appealing and convincing animations. The principles that were developed for traditional animation are equally valid for computer based animation – even if it is just a simple animated banner advertisement.

Squash and stretch

The first principle is **squash and stretch**. All objects, however rigid, have some flexibility and movement when moved. A good example is a bouncing ball, when it hits the floor it squashes slightly as shown in Figure 9.4 and as it flies through the air it stretches out. Clearly the amount an object squashes and stretches dictates how rigid it is. In animations it is important to exaggerate the squashes and stretches so that it is obvious to the viewer what is happening. It is also important to remember that when an object squashes and stretches its volume remains the same otherwise it looks unnatural. When we stretch an object when it is in motion, the stretched object in one frame overlaps with the stretched object in the adjacent frames as shown in Figure 9.5. This is called **motion blur** and helps to create the illusion of speed – remember in cartoons seeing a character's legs become all blurred to indicate speed.

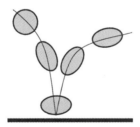

Figure 9.4 A bouncing ball illustrating squash and stretch

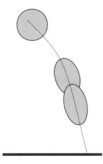

Figure 9.5 The stretched balls in two adjacent frames have overlapped,
creating the effect of motion blur

Timing

The speed with which a piece of action takes place is called **timing** and usually refers to the number of in-between frames in an animation. Correct timing is very important when you want the viewer to see an important action which takes place very quickly. Timing can help to indicate how heavy an object is – if you flicked a balloon it would move very quickly but not very far, whereas if you did the same to an equally sized heavy iron ball, it would move more slowly but further. The balloon's behaviour would be indicated by fewer tweened frames and the iron ball by more. Timing can also help indicate a cartoon character's behaviour, the fewer tweened frames the more frenetic the character's behaviour. For example, a cartoon of a head moving from side to side with many in between frames looks like the character is carefully searching for something; reducing the number of in between frames makes the character look more panicky.

The three phases

There are three phases to a piece of action in an animation: anticipation, staging and then follow through. An animation must be designed so that before an action starts the scene is set so viewers know something is going to happen and also where it is going to happen.

For example, applying the principle of **anticipation** to a banner advertisement where a man is going to bungy-jump off a bridge would mean drawing the viewer's eyes to the top of the bridge by having the man wave his arms in a panic.

Staging involves making sure that action, when it takes place, is clear and unmistakable. In the example of the man bungy-jumping, staging means ensuring that nothing distracts the viewer's eye away from the main action with other actions elsewhere like a seagull flying around. A key technique in staging an action is ensuring that key actions do not take place in front of other actions or they happen in silhouette (i.e. nothing behind the action to cause confusion) so the man falls through a clear blue sky with no clouds.

As an action proceeds there is a **follow through** of associated actions, e.g. as the man falls through the air his arms wave above his head and the elastic rope stretches. Animators often refer to the 'lead' in an action as the part of the animation which initiates and leads the action so as someone walks their hips lead the action and the legs and arms follow through.

Other actions

Actions in animations usually follow **arcs** to make the action seem more natural. Even where an action takes place in a straight line, like the man falling, the fall begins with the man jumping in an arc through the air. When animators try to convey a particular idea it is important to **exaggerate** the idea to ensure the viewer understands. For example, to ensure the viewer understands that the man is panicking at the top of the cliff the waving arms are exaggerated. In facial expressions if a character is sad make him or her sadder, happy – happier, angry – angrier and so on.

A **secondary action** is an action which occurs as a result of the primary action. In the bungy jumper example a seagull flying out of the way would be a secondary action. It is important that secondary actions do not distract from the main action but support it. Animators must be careful to stage secondary actions so that something doesn't go unnoticed like the change of expression on the bungy jumper's face.

The last principle which rests in the skill of the animator as an illustrator is ensuring animations and animation characters have **appeal**. This does not mean always using cute cartoon characters but drawing animations where the viewers are drawn to the idea or action.

--- CRUCIAL CONCEPTS ---

Squash and stretch is the technique of copying and exaggerating the natural behaviour of objects to squash when they come into contact with another object and stretch whey they are moving.
Timing is the technique of determining how many in between frames to use to create different effects. Fewer in between frames makes the animation look more frantic, more makes it look more relaxed.

Quick test

How could the principles of animation be applied to a man falling over?

Section 5

Computer based animation

It is important that you know not only the basics and principles of animation but also how to create animations. Ideally you will get some practice in creating them in your computer workshops.

Animation studios are software programs that allow animators to draw and paint cels, provide key frames with moving backgrounds, use multiple layers for onion skinning, linking to fast video disk recorders for storage and playback and allow scans to be imported directly. Figure 9.6 shows a screen shot of the animation studio called Animation Stand from Linker Systems being used to create an animation of a character walking. Figure 9.6 shows the exposure sheet with each frame running downwards with the objects that appear in each frame placed in the layers running horizontally. Figure 9.6 also shows how the sound track is 'tied' to each frame. Animation studios are generally used to create film quality animations for playing back on television, cinema or video. However the final output could be to Apple's Quicktime or Microsoft's AVI format for playing on a computer.

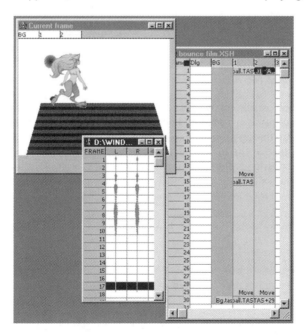

Figure 9.6 Animation Stand being used to create an animation of a cartoon character walking. On the right hand side is the exposure sheet and on the left hand side is the current frame selected in the exposure sheet highlighted in black.

Paint and drawing tools can also be used for creating cel animations. Adobe Photoshop's layers facility can be used for onion skinning by changing each layer's transparency setting to about 50% as shown in Figure 9.7. Vector-based drawing tools like Adobe Illustrator or Macromedia Fireworks can also be used for creating cel animations. Sketches to be used in an animation can be scanned into Adobe Illustrator and then traced and filled using its tools.

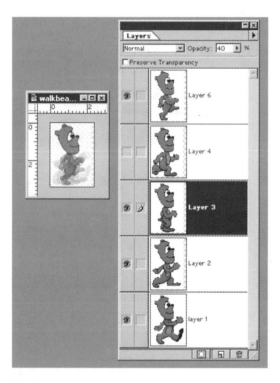

Figure 9.7 Adobe Photoshop with each layer's transparency set to 50% to produce the onion skinning of the image on the left hand side

Perhaps the most common types of animation seen in Web pages are GIF89a images or animated GIFs. **Animated GIFs** are simply a series of static images, i.e. frames in GIF format (see Chapter 8 for an explanation of the GIF image format) bound together with some extra information that tells browsers how to play the animation, like the duration of each frame and the number of times the animation should be played. There are many dedicated tools available to create animated GIFs and most image editing tools like Adobe Photoshop and Jasc Paint Shop Pro have special add-in tools like Adobe Image Ready. Figure 9.2 is a screen shot of an animated GIF taken from Jasc Animation Shop. These tools have special wizards which enable you to automate some aspects of the animation and apply special effects like exploding an image over several frames. The major drawback with animated GIFs is their lack of support for sound, however one of their advantages is that they support transparency so they do not obscure images that lie underneath them in a Web page.

Macromedia Director has evolved over the last decade into the leading multimedia authoring tool. Director is also capable of creating sophisticated animations. Director supports a number of functions to help create animations including:

- tweening between frames including size, position, shape and rotation;
- creation of film loops for applying the cycling technique;
- use of channels and transparency for onion skinning.

Figure 9.8 shows Director being used to create an animation of a ball bouncing down some steps. You can see that a film loop of the spinning ball and its path down the steps has already been created. On the left hand side of Figure 9.8 is Director's 'Stage' which shows the objects (referred to in Director as sprites) in the animation. On the right hand side of Figure 9.8 is Director's 'Score' where each frame is represented by a vertical column and the horizontal channels represent the objects or sprites. The bouncing ball is located in channel 1 and each step is represented in channels 2-6. Animations created in Director are played by converting them into an executable 'projector' file. A special plug in called the Shockwave Player needs to be installed into the browser before it is possible to see Director animations in Web pages.

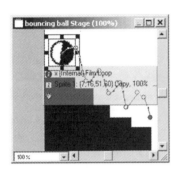
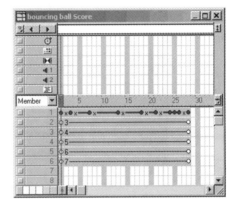

Figure 9.8 Macromedia Director being used to create an animation of a ball bouncing down some steps. The ball itself is a 'film loop' so it spins as it bounces

In the last few years **Macromedia Flash** has become an important tool for creating real time animations for Web pages. Macromedia Flash is vector based so it means it can produce animations with small file sizes. Flash also supports sound. Flash is similar to Director in that it uses a score to create animations. Figure 9.9 shows a screen shot of Flash also being used to create an animation of a bouncing ball. Since Flash is vector based, animators still create the key frames but Flash generates the tweened frames themselves at run time. A special plug in called the Flash Player needs to be installed into the browser before it is possible to see Flash animations in Web pages.

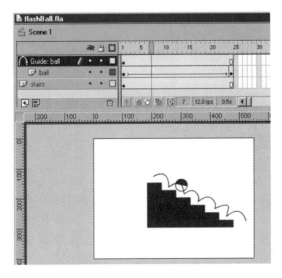

Figure 9.9 Macromedia Flash being used to recreate the bouncing ball. Flash is capable of tweening the rotation of the bouncing ball and its path

Simple animations can be now be created in Web pages using something called **dynamic HTML** (see Chapters 12 and 13 for an explanation of HTML and dynamic HTML) which involves adding programming code using a scripting language called Javascript. The bouncing ball shown in Figure 9.10 was developed in Macromedia Dreamweaver – one of the leading DHTML development tools. Notice the similarity to Director and Flash to create the bouncing ball animation. Animated GIFs can be combined with dynamic HTML to produce more sophisticated animations. The advantage of using dynamic HTML is that it doesn't require a plug in but the disadvantage is that the level of control over the animation is limited.

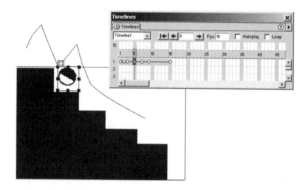

Figure 9.10 Macromedia Dreamweaver being used to recreate the bouncing ball.
The path of animated objects can only move in straight lines in DHTML

CRUCIAL CONCEPTS

Animation studios are tools used to create cel animations.
Paint and drawing tools can be used to create cel animations using layers and transparency options.
Animated GIFs are a simple frame by frame animation format used extensively in Web pages.

Quick test

What tool would you use to create a cartoon animation for (i) television and (ii) Web pages?

Section 6

3D animation

With the arrival of powerful desktop computers it is now possible to produce quite effective 3D animations on a small scale, like animated 3D logos. In this chapter we briefly cover some of the key principles of 3D animation and the desktop level tools available. For a full consideration of 3D animation see References at the end of this chapter.

3D animations are based on a coordinate system with three axes as you might have studied in your mathematics courses and shown in Figure 9.11. All objects in a 3D animation are defined in terms of their x, y and z coordinates. The process of 3D animation involves four stages, modelling, scene building, rendering and animation.

In the **modelling** stage each object is slowly constructed using the functions of the 3D modelling tool. For example to build a 3D dumbbell would require the animator to construct two spheres, then the bar which joins them and then finally 'glue' the three bits together to form the dumbbell. 3D modelling can be confusing because objects are modelled as 'wire frames', as shown in Figure 9.12, so when objects become sufficiently complex it becomes difficult to discern what the object is.

Modelling tools contain various techniques for constructing objects the most common ones are:

- extrusion;
- revolving;
- sweeping;
- Booleans and deformations.

Extrusion involves taking a 2D shape like a triangle and extending it in the third dimension as shown in Figure 9.13(a).

Revolving involves drawing a 2D object like a circle and revolving it about the third axis to form a doughnut shape as shown in Figure 9.13(b).

Sweeping is similar to extrusion only the line of extrusion can be a curve, as shown in Figure 9.13(c).

Booleans are shapes formed by the interactions of two or more objects, Figure 9.14(a) shows how two new shapes can be created by the interaction of a cube and a sphere. Figure 9.14(b) is called an intersection, and Figure 9.14(c) is called a union. 3D models can also be deformed in many different ways, including squashing, stretching and bending.

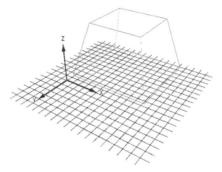

Figure 9.11 3D coordinate system

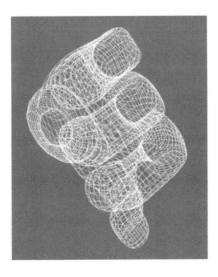

Figure 9.12 3D wire frame model

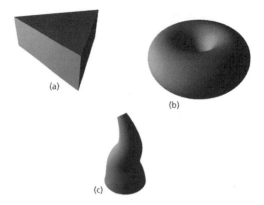

Figure 9.13 (a) An example of a triangle extruded, (b) an example of a circle revolved about an axis and (c) a circle swept along a curve

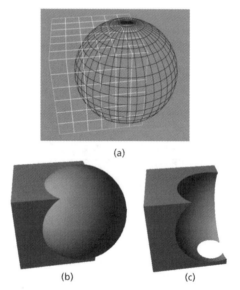

Figure 9.14 (a) A wire frame sphere and cube, (b) an intersection of the sphere and cube rendered, (c) a union of the sphere and cube rendered

Once the required 3D models are complete the scene can be built. **Scene building** involves positioning and scaling all the objects to their right location in the 3D scene which would also have been built prior to this stage.

The next stage is called **rendering**. Rendering is analogous to applying paint and makes the wire frame objects look solid. When the scene was constructed a simple shade render would have been applied to the objects to remove viewing problems. Once the scene has been built the simple shade render is removed and a more realistic render applied. Realistic render takes into account the texture of objects (rough or smooth, etc.), lighting (direction and intensity), and atmosphere (damp, misty, clear, etc.). Applying lighting effects is a very skilled task and to be convincing requires sophisticated software. Lighting will probably come from more than one source and these have to be reproduced in the scene.

The final stage is the **animation** of the 3D model and is very similar to its 2D counterpart described above. The animation stage involves setting up key frames and then applying tweening techniques to create the in-between frames, this process is helped by the fact that the 3D model is vector based.

CRUCIAL CONCEPTS

3D modelling is the process of constructing a 3D object using techniques like extrusion, revolving, sweeping, applying boolean transformations and deformation.
3D animation is similar to the 2D process of key frames and tweening.

CRUCIAL TIP

Unless you are on a specialist course it is unlikely you will do much 3D animation since it is time consuming and resource intensive. However you should be familiar with the general approach and some of the commonly available 3D animation tools.

Quick test

What are the various techniques used to construct 3D models?

Section 7

End of chapter assessment

Multiple choice questions

1. Which of the following statements is true of the value of animation?
    a) provide interesting distractions
    b) reduce the level of communication
    c) increase understanding
    d) demonstrate the developer's skill.

2. Which of the following statements is true of frames in animation?
    a) the colour depth should be set as high as possible
    b) the frame rate should be kept above ten per second
    c) the frame size should be 100 by 100 pixels
    d) the frame rate for Web-based animations is important.

3. Which statement is true of cel animations?
    a) the height and width proportions of story boards are not important
    b) onion skinning ensures only the active frame is visible
    c) the technique of limited animation increases the file size
    d) maintaining volume is important in applying squash and stretch.

4. In the principles of animation which of these is true?
    a) exaggeration should not be used
    b) motion blur can be created by applying 'follow through'
    c) motion blur can be created by applying squash and stretch
    d) changing the frame rate has no effect on the 'timing' of a piece of animation.

5. In computer based animation which of these is true?
    a) paint and drawing tools are not used
    b) dynamic HTML supports limited tweening
    c) animated GIFS support sound
    d) animation studios provide limited support for creating animations.

6. In 3D animation which of these is true?
   a) rendering is the technique of construction a 3D object
   b) scene building involving extruding 3D objects
   c) 3D modelling involves tweening between key frames
   d) final rendering should consider lighting and atmospheric effects.

Multiple choice answers

1. c)   2. d)   3. d)   4. c)   5. b)   6. d)

Questions

1. How and why would you use animation to help you advertise an online book store?
2. Explain with reference to an example how a computer-based frame animation is created including the technique of tweening.
3. What techniques can you apply to ensure that an animation is realistic and convincing?
4. How would you go about creating a CD-ROM based animation that explained how a computer worked. What tools would you use and why?
5. Explain the stages involved in creating a 3D animation of a company logo.

Answers

1. The points that need to be included in the answer are:
   - An animated advertisement is more likely to attract attention compared to static advertisements.
   - An animated advertisement is more likely to maintain the attention of the viewer using techniques like anticipation, timing and staging.
   - It is possible to explain the details of more complex products more easily.
   - You should explain the difference between using an animated GIF and a Flash application to create this animation and perhaps the problems of the size limitations of a banner advertisement.

2. You need to pick a simple example like a bouncing ball, something falling, or flying through the air. With reference to the example the answer would explain:
   - How storyboards are used to generate and communicate ideas.
   - Key frames mark the beginning and end images of a piece of animation action with an example drawing of a beginning and end key frame.
   - The tweened frames need to be created to show the animation moving from the start key frame to the end key frame with an example tweened frame.
   - Some tools supported onion skinning so designers can see all the frames in the animation sequence semi-transparently on top of each other to check the flow of the animation.
   - An animation studio could be used if the tweened frames were going to be drawn manually one at a time, or if the tweened frames are going to be automatically generated, Macromedia Flash or Director could be used.
   - The key frames could either be drawn by hand and scanned in or drawn using a paint or drawing tool like Adobe Photoshop or Adobe Illustrator and imported into an animation studio like Animation Stand.

3. Your answer needs to systematically work through an explanation of the following concepts and why they help to make an animation appear more convincing:
   - squash and stretch;
   - motion blur;

- timing;
- anticipation;
- staging;
- exaggerate;
- secondary action;
- appeal.

4. This question gives you plenty of opportunity to demonstrate your understanding of the principles and techniques involved in creating animations. The points you should include in your answer are:

- The importance of storyboarding the animation.

- The identification of the key action sequences, e.g. data moving from memory to CPU.

- The drawing of the key frames with an explanation that these can be done by hand or using a paint or drawing tool or even using an animation studio.

- An explanation that the tweened frames are required and how these could be created, e.g. by hand or automated using tools like Flash or Director.

- An explanation of how the principles of animation could be applied with an example, e.g. the use of 'timing' to show the speed data travels around the motherboard.

- The format of the animation to be included on the CD-ROM. If it includes sound then it can not be an animated GIF. Could the whole animation be completed in Flash or Director, or if an animation studio is being used how can its format be converted into QuickTime or Microsoft AVI formats?

- You could discuss how 3D animation techniques could be used.

- You could also discuss how the animation could be made interactive.

5. The answer might start with discussing a simple 2D representation of a logo, e.g. an acronym like 'GJE' and showing how the various modelling techniques might be applied to make the acronym 3D, e.g. extrusion, Boolean. You might want to explain the use of three coordinates to define a 3D object. You might try drawing examples of the application of the modelling techniques although obviously this will not be as easy as drawing in 2D. The answer should then explain how a shade render is used to make the 3D model easy to see by hiding the wire frame appearance.

The answer should now explain the scene building stage and the process of positioning and scaling the 3D models. In the example of the logo you might explain that each letter is modelled separately and brought together but not obviously as part of an acronym. Each letter might be rotated, positioned away from each other and not in the order G, J and then E.

The answer should then explain how the final render is added and how lighting and atmospheric effects are taken into consideration. The final part of the answer points out that animating a 3D model is similar to 2D animation utilising key frames and generating tweened frames.

Section 8

Further reading

Giambruno, M. (2002) *3D Graphics and Animation,* New Riders.
Wagstaff, S. (1999) *Animation on the Web*, Peachpit.

Chapter 10
Audio

Chapter summary

In this chapter we look at the theory and principles of audio digitisation and use. Audio is likely to play an important supporting role in many multimedia applications.

Learning outcomes

After studying this chapter you should aim to achieve these targets by answering the questions at the end of the chapter. You should be able to:

Outcome 1: **Recognise the different reasons that audio may be used in a multimedia application.**
Outcome 2: **Understand the process of digitising an analogue sound wave and the technical choices associated with digitisation.**
Outcome 3: **Understand the differences between Digital Audio and MIDI.**

How will you be assessed on this?

In an exam you may be asked to explain the ways in which audio can be used in multimedia applications. You may be asked to explain the process of digitising audio and the technical choices facing the multimedia developer. You may be asked to identify possible sources of audio material and to show an awareness of the IPR implications of using or creating material (see Chapter 4).

In coursework that required you to build a multimedia application, you might be expected to explain your reasons for using audio in a particular way within the application. You will be expected to justify the decisions you have made when digitising and manipulating audio. It is likely that you will need to gather or create source material which is suitable for your application. You may also need to consider the IPR implications of using material.

Section 1

Using audio in multimedia applications

This section outlines the reasons why audio is used in multimedia applications and the different effects that audio might achieve.

─── CRUCIAL CONCEPTS ───
Audio is particularly useful for provoking an **emotional response** from users. Audio may form part of the **content** of our application, it may form part of the **interface**, or it may simply be **incidental** as part of the background.

When creating multimedia applications, one of the effects we wish to achieve is provoking an emotional response from the user. We may wish to shock the user, or build up tension and anticipation. All the media assets are capable of generating an emotional response in the user but sound is particularly effective. Sound can of course be used for other reasons besides invoking an emotional response. Sound can be a very resource intensive medium and you will need to consider when it is appropriate to use it in your application and what quality of sound is required.

Within multimedia applications sound is typically used in combination with another medium and only occasionally by itself. This is partly due to the dominance of the visual element in multimedia applications, users expect to have something to look at even when they are listening to sound. It is also partly due to the fact that sound works well in reinforcing information presented visually, but has limitations when used by itself. For instance it is very easy to scan through a page of text to relocate a particular section, it is less easy to scan through a recording containing a spoken version of the text.

The process of professional quality sound production and recording requires specialist skills and equipment. As a result of this, it may be contracted out to an external company.

Audio can be loosely classified according to type:

- **Speech** – recorded voices.
- **Music** – recorded from the real world or synthesised.
- **Other real world sounds** – recorded real world sounds such as animal calls or traffic noise.
- **Synthesised sounds** – such as beeps and whooshes on a computer.

Audio can also be classified according to the way it is used within a multimedia application.

Content audio communicates content to the user. It can be used in a variety of situations:

- **Narration** – recorded voice is used to present the subject matter. Narration will often be used in combination with another medium, for example to describe a process being shown in an animation. The voice talent (the person whose voice is recorded) used for the narration is not important.

- **Testimonials** – the recorded voice of a specific person, often from a particular occasion, is used to present their opinions. In some cases the distinction between a narration and a testimonial is blurred, for example if a well known personality is used as the voice talent for a narration.

- **Music and recorded sounds** – particular pieces of music or particular recorded sounds which form part of the subject matter.

Lengthy sound files, in particular narration and testimonials, should be used sparingly within a multimedia application. Voice clips should typically be kept short and should be integrated with complementary media. Voice clips are useful in situations where it is important to convey the affective state (e.g. happy) or illocutionary force (e.g. urgent), or where the speaker's accent or age enhances the information presentation.

Interface audio is typically associated with elements of the interface, such as buttons:

- **Voice-overs** – narration can be used to provide short instructions.
- **Feedback** – sound effects can be used to reinforce visual feedback on user actions, such as an audible 'click' when the user presses a button.
- **Alerts** – audio is an effective way of attracting the user's attention, but is less good for longer warning messages unless the user has the option to replay them.

Incidental audio does not directly inform the user, but can be used to reinforce elements of the presentation or to make the presentation more aesthetically pleasing:

- **Message reinforcing background sounds** – the use of background sounds that relate to the subject. Although the sound is related to the subject matter, it does not directly form part of it.
- **Mood generating background sounds and music** – these are similar to message reinforcing sounds, but have the specific intention of invoking a particular mood or emotion in the user. The distinction between this type of sound and content sound can sometimes be hard to draw.
- **Period setting background sounds or music** – this type of background sound is designed to invoke a particular historical time.
- **Time setting background sounds or music** – this type of background sound is intended to invoke a particular time of day.
- **Geographical setting background sounds or music** – these are background sounds which invoke a particular country or place.
- **Location enhancing sounds** – sound can be used to give a greater sense of physical location.
- **General background sounds** – music can be used as a general background.

Given the numerous opportunities for using sound, you may be tempted to include a large number of sound files within your multimedia application. There are several good reasons for avoiding this temptation:

- Overuse of audio, particularly incidental interface and ambient audio, can be irritating for the user once the novelty wears off. The user may then turn the sound down and therefore not hear other important audio such as instructions or content.
- Audio files can occupy a large quantity of storage space or bandwidth, leaving less for other digital assets.
- Support for audio on older PC platforms is variable. An application that relies very heavily on audio may not be usable if audio support is either limited or unavailable.

Quick test

1. Is audio the only medium that will generate an emotional response in the user?
2. What are the three main uses for audio within a multimedia application?

Section 2

The physics of sound

In this section we briefly examine the physics of sound. Although you do not need to understand the physics of sound in order to include it in your multimedia application, it is useful to be familiar with the basic terminology and principles. It will also help you understand some of the technical choices facing you when digitising and working with audio.

CRUCIAL CONCEPTS

Sound travels in **waves** which can be described in terms of their **amplitude** (loudness) and **frequency** (pitch).

In nature, sound travels in the form of continuous analogue **waves** made up of compressed and expanded air molecules, similar to the waves caused by throwing a stone into a pond. Complex waveforms are composed of a number of simpler waveforms each of which takes the form of a sine wave.

Each sine wave can be described in terms of its peak height (**amplitude**) and the number of repeated cycles per second (**frequency**). A **cycle** is defined as part of the wave starting at zero amplitude, reaching a peak of maximum positive amplitude, passing through zero amplitude again, reaching a trough of maximum negative amplitude and returning again to zero amplitude (Figure 10.1).

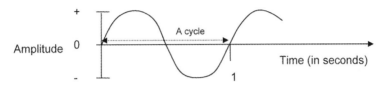

Figure 10.1 A wave with a 1Hz frequency

When two waves exist at the same time and in the same place, they will combine to form a new wave form (Figures 10.2, 10.3 and 10.4).

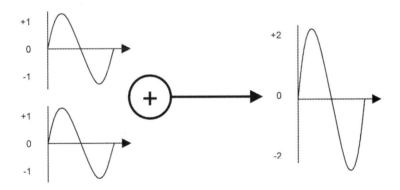

Figure 10.2 Two waves combining to form a new wave

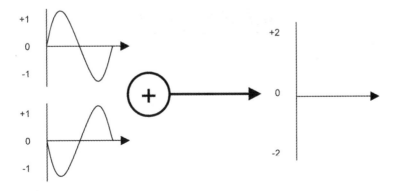

Figure 10.3 Two waves cancelling each other out

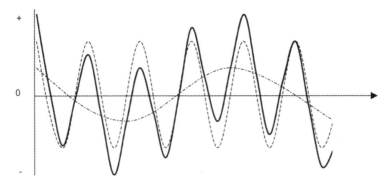

Figure 10.4 Two waves (dashed) combining to form new wave (bold)

Differences in the maximum positive (or negative) **amplitude** between two waves are perceived as differences in **loudness**. The wave with the larger amplitude will be perceived as the louder.

The amplitude or acoustic power of a wave is measured in acoustic watts. The range of sounds that a human can perceive is from approximately 0.000000000001 to 10 acoustic watts. For convenience a logarithmic scale expressed in decibels, dB, is typically used. The dB scale is a better model of the way humans perceive changes in loudness. The softest sound that a human ear can detect is defined as 0 dB. A change of 1 dB represents the smallest difference that can be detected by a trained listener. The average listener can only detect a change of around 3 dB, a doubling of power. In order for the listener to perceive a doubling of loudness, the power must be increased by 10 dB. The point at which a sound is so loud that it is painful, and hearing loss may result, is around 130 dB.

Acoustic watts	dB	
0.000000000001	0	threshold of hearing
0.0000000001	20	quiet livingroom background
0.0000001	50	average office background
0.000001	60	average conversation
0.001	90	shouted conversation
1.0	120	pneumatic drill
10.0	130	threshold of pain

Figure 10.5 Acoustic watts and decibels

The **frequency** of a sound is perceived as **pitch**, a sound with a higher frequency being perceived as being higher pitched than one with a lower frequency. Frequency is a physical measurement, whilst pitch is perceived, the relationship is not direct. The frequency of a sound is expressed in terms of the number of times the cycle is repeated per second and is measured in Hertz, Hz, though this will often be expressed in kilo Hertz, kHz, where 1 kHz is a thousand cycles per second. The human ear can detect frequencies in the range 20 Hz to 17 kHz, the upper limit diminishing to 15 kHz or lower with age or damage.

Amplitude does not depend on frequency. Two waves with different frequencies can have the same amplitude and vice versa (Figures 10.6 and 10.7). The perception of loudness depends on the frequency of the sound and the characteristics of the listener's hearing.

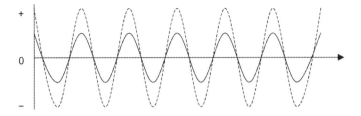

Figure 10.6 Two waves, same frequency, different amplitude

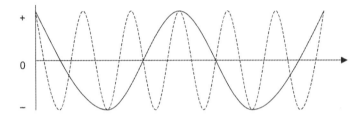

Figure 10.7 Two waves, different frequency, same amplitude

Remember, real world sound waves are complex combinations of waves (Figure 10.8). The fundamental frequency of a sound is augmented by harmonics at integer multiples of that frequency, e.g. twice the frequency, three times the frequency. The combination of harmonics at different amplitudes varies according to the individual instrument used to generate the sound. This is why the same note played on different instruments sounds different. The combination of frequencies produced by an instrument or voice is known as the **timbre** or **tone colour**.

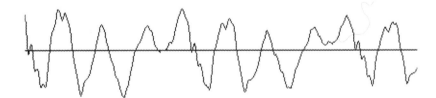

Figure 10.8 Example of a real sound wave

In addition to pitch and loudness the brain is able to interpret sound to provide three-dimensional location (where a sound is coming from) and movement information (the direction in which a sound source is moving relative to our position).

Quick test

1. What is the amplitude of a sound perceived as?

2. What is the frequency of a sound perceived as?

3. How many cycles per second is 20 kHz?

4. What is timbre?

Digital Audio and digitisation

In this section we outline the process of digitising a sound wave so that it can be manipulated and delivered in multimedia applications.

─────────── CRUCIAL CONCEPTS ───────────

Digital Audio is a digitised representation of a sound wave. The wave is **sampled** and the sample values **quantized** to create the digital representation. The process of digitisation can introduce errors, such as **aliasing** (when too few samples are taken), **quantization** errors (where continuous values are mapped to a discrete scale) and **clipping** (when amplitudes are truncated).

As with all our media assets, the sound that we use in our multimedia application will need to be in digital form. As far as digital sound is concerned there are two very different formats, Digital Audio (DA) and Musical Instrument Digital Interface (MIDI). **Digital Audio** is a digitised representation of analogue sound waves, whilst **MIDI** is a form of programming language for synthesisers. MIDI will be discussed in Section 5.

Digital Audio involves the conversion of the continuous analogue sound wave into a digital approximation of that sound wave. Essentially the shape of the sound wave is represented digitally. During playback of the sound it is converted back into analogue form.

The conversion from an analogue wave to a digital representation of that wave (digitisation) involves two processes – sampling and quantization. In **sampling** (also known as **time discretisation**) the analogue amplitude values are captured at regular intervals along the time axis of the analogue sound wave (Figure 10.9).

The number of samples taken per second is referred to as the **sampling rate** or **sampling frequency**. This is typically expressed in kHz, 'thousand samples per second', but the sampling rate is not directly related to the frequency of the sound being sampled. Typical sampling rates for multimedia are 44.1 kHz, 22.05 kHz and 11.025 kHz, commonly referred to as 44 kHz, 22 kHz and 11 kHz. The higher the sampling rate, the better quality the digitised sound will be.

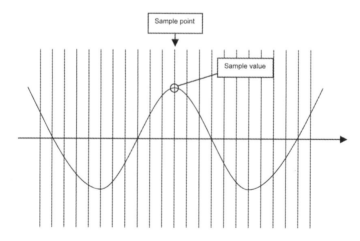

Figure 10.9 Sampling a wave at regular intervals

In **quantization** (also known as **amplitude discretisation**) the sampled analogue values are approximated by digital values taken from a limited range of discrete values (Figure 10.10).

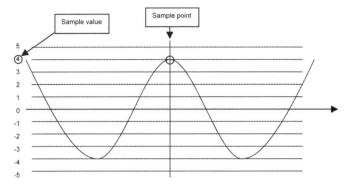

Figure 10.10 Quantization of the sampled value

The range of discrete values that can be used to approximate the actual sampled analogue value is referred to as the **sample depth** or **sample resolution**. Typical sample depths are 8-bit (256 values) or 16-bit (65,536 values).

The sampling rate and sample depth are crucial factors in the quality of the digital representation and in the size of the resulting sound file. The higher the sampling rate and the larger the sample depth, the more accurate the digital approximation will be and therefore the more faithful the reproduction of the sound will be. However, as the number of samples and the depth of the samples increase, so does the size of the sound file.

Stereo sound is composed of two very similar sound waves. The subtle differences result in the perception of location and movement. For stereo sound you must record a separate sound wave for each channel, therefore your sound file will be twice the size. As **mono** uses only one channel of sound, using it can be a good way to keep sound files small. As a general rule, you should use mono where possible and certainly in cases where there is little or no benefit in using stereo, such as:

- when the original sound source is in mono;
- if the delivery platform only supports basic audio;
- if the delivery platform has poorly positioned stereo speakers;
- for voice recordings;
- for simple interface sounds;
- when the sampling rate used is 11 kHz or less, as the distinction between stereo and mono is lost.

The size of a digitised sound recording in bytes is given by:

file size = duration of recording in seconds × number of samples per second × size of each sample × number of channels (1 or 2).

In other words:

file size in bytes = duration of recording in seconds × sample rate × (sample depth in bits ÷ 8) × (1 or 2).

For example, for a 20 second recording at 22 kHz sample rate, 16-bit sample depth, mono (one channel), we get:

20 × 22050 × (16 ÷ 8) × 1 = 882,000 bytes.

─────────── CRUCIAL TIP ───────────

Remember 22 kHz is not 22000 samples per second, it is 22050 samples per second. 22 kHz is just shorthand notation.

The conversion of an analogue wave into a digital form is necessarily an approximation, and can be seen as distorting the original sound. The choice of sampling rate and sample depth can introduce or compound certain types of distortion, namely aliasing, quantization errors and clipping.

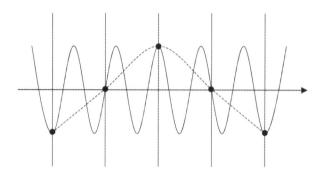

Figure 10.11 Aliasing (dashed) when too few samples are taken

Aliasing occurs if the sampling rate is too low and too few samples are taken, when the digital approximation will not accurately represent the original wave (Figure 10.11).

In order to avoid aliasing, a sample must be taken at least twice per cycle, so the sampling rate must be at least twice as high as the highest frequency that is to be recorded. This is known as the Nyquist limit. One approach to avoiding aliasing is to ensure that frequencies beyond the Nyquist limit, given a particular sample rate, are not recorded; a filter is used to remove them before the analogue to digital conversion. An alternative solution is oversampling. Initially the sound is sampled at very high rates, many times higher than the highest frequency in the sound. The digital information is then filtered to remove problematic frequencies that would cause problems at lower sample rates. The digital information is then resampled at a lower sample rate for storage and editing.

Quantization errors are distortions that occur during the conversion between a continuous range of amplitude values in the analogue wave and the fixed number provided by the sample depth. The actual continuous amplitude values are replaced by the nearest available digital value (Figure 10.12). This can introduce a hissing sound into the audio. A 16-bit sample depth greatly reduces this quantization noise when compared to an 8-bit sample depth.

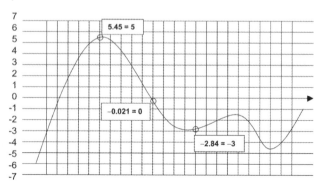

Figure 10.12 Quantization errors when continuous values are approximated

Clipping occurs when the analogue wave contains amplitudes that are beyond the range that can be represented by the sample depth (Figure 10.13). These amplitudes are replaced by the closest value available within the sample depth. Clipping can cause serious distortions in audio. Clipping can also be introduced due to limitations in the hardware used during the recording process.

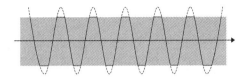

Figure 10.13 Clipping errors when amplitudes are truncated (dashed)

Quick test

1. What are typical sampling rates and which result in higher quality digitisation?
2. What are typical sample depths and which result in higher quality digitisation?
3. What are the formulae for calculating the size of a mono and stereo Digital Audio file?
4. When should mono be used in preference to stereo?

Section 4

Digital Audio software

In this section we will be considering what general facilities sound capture and editing software possess. When you start using such software it is useful to understand the more theoretical aspects covered in previous sections.

Often facilities for capturing Digital Audio will be combined with those for editing it within a single piece of software. Typical operations include:

• capturing sound from pre-recorded sources or live via a microphone	• cross fading – fading two sounds into each other to avoid large changes in amplitude
• selecting sample rates and sizes and mono/stereo when capturing sound	• resampling or downsampling – reducing the sampling rates and depths to reduce file size
• file format conversion – converting sound files from one file format to another	• fade-in and fade-out – to fade sounds in and out
• trimming – removing blank space from the recording	• digital signal processing filters – applies special effects, such as reverberation
• cutting and pasting – selecting sounds and combining them to form new sounds	• changing the time dimension – reversing the sound, making it faster or slower
• converting stereo to mono	• viewing the waveform at various levels of resolution
• volume adjustments – so that individual sounds have the same playback volume.	• more sophisticated tools will allow different sounds to be placed in separate channels so that they can be edited independently.

Whilst editing Digital Audio it is important to use the highest quality sound possible. Every time an editing operation is performed on the sound file there is the potential for losing data. It is also important to be aware that applying a filter to a 44 kHz sample and converting to 11 kHz may result in a better sound than that achieved by converting the sample to 11 kHz and then applying the filter. It can also be useful to preserve a high quality archive copy of your sound files for future development work, along with the original source material.

Digital Audio can be hard to compress effectively, particularly 16-bit audio, and the human ear is very sensitive to data loss. Typically, much of the data reduction in Digital Audio is achieved through reduced sampling rate and depth and the use of mono in place of stereo.

One popular audio **compression** scheme is MPEG audio, which includes MP3. It is a **lossy compression**, i.e. the signal resulting after the decompression is not identical to the original signal as data has been discarded during the compression process. However, MPEG is based on psychoacoustic principles, irrelevant and redundant parts of the signal (based on how the brain perceives sound) are removed, resulting in a perceptually lossless compression (people can't hear the difference). Compression ratios of around 10:1 are achievable, with no perceptible quality loss. MPEG typically requires hardware assistance for compressing, but can be decompressed in software.

One possibility we may consider, especially if our application will be delivered over a network, is **streaming audio**. In non-streaming audio the whole audio file must be downloaded before the audio can be played. Streaming audio plays the audio as it arrives. This reduces waiting times and also means that the entire audio file is never stored on the user's machine. Streaming audio often requires special server software.

Quick test

What types of operation would a typical sound editing software package provide?

Section 5

MIDI – Musical Instrument Digital Interface

In this section we outline the principles behind MIDI (Musical Instrument Digital Interface).

--- CRUCIAL CONCEPT ---

MIDI (Musical Instrument Digital Interface) allows compatible synthesiser devices to be controlled and played using instructions.

Musical Instrument Digital Interface (MIDI) defines a communication standard for electronic musical instruments and computers. MIDI is a hardware standard (cables, circuits, electronic signals) and a data communication standard (types and formats of messages). MIDI does not involve the storage of sound, rather it stores binary instructions, which are used to control MIDI devices which generate the required sound. **MIDI devices** come in a variety of forms:

- **instrument-based synthesisers** – keyboards, drum machines and similar instrument-based interface;
- **sound modules** – synthesisers without an instrument-based interface;
- **plug-in cards** – which contain synthesisers for computers;
- **software based synthesisers** – for computers.

MIDI devices have a number of characteristics:

- **Timbral palette** – the number of different instrument voices a device can play.
- **Multi-timbral capacity** – most MIDI devices can play several instrument voices simultaneously, each of which can respond to a single MIDI channel.
- **Polyphony capacity** – refers to the ability of a device to play more than one note on an instrument voice at one time.

MIDI messages are composed of three elements:

- **device number** – identifies which MIDI device the message is for;
- **control segment** – for instance to turn on a particular synthesiser circuit;
- **data segment** – action to be performed, volume, etc.

MIDI is device dependent. Channel 1 may be different instruments on different MIDI systems, so MIDI cannot be guaranteed to sound the same on different systems. **General MIDI** is a standard for consumer level synthesisers that identifies a basic common set of 128 MIDI instruments, known as the Instrument Patch Map. Although General MIDI compatible MIDI files will sound similar on different General MIDI devices, there is still no guarantee of identical reproduction, as the standard does not specify the way in which the sounds are to be synthesised.

Some applications will involve a combination of both MIDI and Digital Audio formats, each being used where it is appropriate. In other cases MIDI will be used for the creation and editing of music, but the music will be recorded and converted to Digital Audio for delivery in the multimedia application.

Quick test

What is the main difference between Digital Audio and MIDI?

Section 6

End of chapter assessment

Multiple choice questions

1. When two sound waves exist at the same time and in the same place, they will usually –
   a) cancel each other out
   b) get louder
   c) form a new wave
   d) raise the pitch.

2. A two-minute sound clip is sampled at 22 kHz, 8-bit, stereo. The size of the resulting sound file in bytes is –
   a) 2646000
   b) 88200
   c) 5292000
   d) 5280000
   e) 42336000.

3. Aliasing occurs when –

   a) the sampling rate is too high
   b) the sample depth is too low
   c) the sample depth is too high
   d) the sampling rate is too low.

4. Which statement best describes MIDI?

   a) a digitised wave form
   b) a set of musical notes
   c) a sequence of digital samples
   d) a set of instructions.

Multiple choice answers

1. c) is the right answer, though any of the others may also happen in specific circumstances.

2. c) is the right answer. If you calculated a) remember to multiply by 2 for stereo. If you calculated b) remember to convert to seconds. If you calculated d) remember it is 22050 and not 22000. If you calculated e) remember to divide by 8 to give bytes.

3. d) is the right answer.

4. d) is the right answer.

Questions

1. Suggest reasons why the text of Martin Luther King's 'I have a dream' speech might be used in a multimedia application in preference to an original sound recording.

2. A multimedia development team has discovered that the sound element of their production is too large for delivery on CD-ROM. The sound has been sampled at 44 kHz, with a 16-bit sample size, and is in stereo. Discuss the different ways in which the storage requirements of the sound can be reduced, alternatives that can be proposed, and the circumstances in which they are appropriate.

3. Describe the process of converting analogue sound into Digital Audio, explain particularly the meaning of the terms 'sampling rate', 'sample depth', 'aliasing', 'clipping' and 'quantization error'.

Answers

1. We are being asked to *suggest reasons why we might use the text of Martin Luther King's 'I have a dream' speech in preference to an original sound recording*. When thinking about our answer we can consider the general case of why we might prefer text to audio, and any specific reasons relating to the particular clip under discussion. We can also make some assumptions about ways the speech might be used in the application. We will need to draw information from Chapter 4 on IPR to fully answer this question. Some reasons we might give are:

   • Our users may want to study the speech in detail, this is easier when using text than audio.
   • Our users may want to compare the speech with another speech or another written source, this is easier when using text than audio.
   • The storage or bandwidth requirement for the audio will be more than for the text.
   • The original audio recording may be of poor quality.
   • The IPR for the audio may cost more to license than the IPR for the text.

- We may wish to play some other audio whilst the user reads the speech, perhaps to set the atmosphere.
- The delivery platform may not support audio, or the application may be installed in a noisy environment.

2. We are being asked to *discuss ways of reducing the storage requirements, alternatives that can be proposed*, and the *circumstances in which they are appropriate*. The first thing that we should discuss is that the current sampling rate and sample depth are both high and that stereo is being used. Obvious ways of reducing the storage requirements are to reduce the sampling rate to 22 kHz or 11 kHz, to reduce the sample depth to 8 bit and to use mono instead of stereo. We could illustrate the reduction this would make, using the formula for calculating the size of a Digital Audio file. However, our answer needs to go beyond this.

We need to consider whether the associated loss of quality is acceptable for the application. As we are not told what the application is, we could give examples of the types of audio that could be made smaller without compromising their quality too much and those that cannot. It may be that the best approach for the application is to preserve some of the audio at the current high quality, but to reduce others to save storage space. We could also simply look at reducing the amount of audio in the application.

We should also mention compression. Whilst we might mention particular compression schemes by name if we remember any, we can still talk about compression in general if not.

Another possibility is to deliver any musical content in MIDI format, though we are not told enough about the application or delivery platform to know if this is a good solution.

3. We are being asked to *describe the process of digitisation* and to *explain the meaning of 'sampling rate', 'sample depth, 'aliasing', 'clipping' and 'quantization error'*. Because the question asks us to explain certain terms, it contains useful reminders about the process of digitisation.

Essentially digitisation involves the approximation of an analogue sound wave by a series of digital values. Samples are taken at regular time intervals as specified by the sampling rate, and the amplitude of the sound wave at that time point is approximated by the nearest discrete value. Sample depth refers to the number of discrete values and is similar to resolution in an image. We can use an illustration similar to Figure 10.9 or 10.10 to clarify this description. We should mention the relationship between quality and file size and the formula for calculating the size of a file.

We should then explain what the three types of error are, why they occur and what steps can be taken to prevent them occurring. It would be useful to include drawings similar to Figures 10.11, 10.12 and 10.13 to illustrate our explanation.

Section 7

Further reading and research

Reading

Bartlett, B. and Bartlett, J. (1998) *Practical Recording Techniques*, Focal Press.
Beggs, J. and Thede, D. (2001) *Designing Web Audio*, O'Reilly.
Huber, D.M. and Runstein, R.E. (2001) *Modern Recording Techniques*, Focal Press.

Research

Your learning resources centre may have collections of copyright free or licensed audio. Find out about these – what conditions are there on their use, what format are they in, how are they categorised? This will be a useful resource when you are developing your applications. You should also look for reputable sources of audio on the Web (such as creative.gettyimages.com) as some of these have collections of rights free material. Be sure that the source is reputable as there are many sites which offer media which they claim are copyright free but are in fact not.

Your learning resources centre will have audio equipment that you can borrow. Practise with the equipment before you have to use it for an assignment.

Flick through different music stations on your radio. For each piece of music you hear, try to form an impression of the message the music conveys – happy, sad, formal, exciting. You can do a similar thing with music in shops – what is the music trying to tell you about the shop?

Chapter 11
Video

Chapter summary

This chapter describes the theory and principles of video digitisation and the use of video in multimedia applications. Video places considerable demands on current technology but is likely to play an increasingly important role in future multimedia applications.

Learning outcomes

After studying this chapter you should aim to achieve these targets by answering the questions at the end of the chapter. You should be able to:

> Outcome 1: **Recognise the different reasons that video may be used in a multimedia application.**
> Outcome 2: **Understand the process of digitising video and the technical choices associated with digitisation.**

How will you be assessed on this?

In an exam you may be asked to explain the ways in which video is being used in multimedia applications. You may be asked to explain the process of digitising video and the technical choices and difficulties facing the multimedia developer when using video. You may be asked to identify possible sources of video material and to show an awareness of the IPR implications of using or creating material (see Chapter 4).

In coursework that required you to build a multimedia application, you might be expected to explain your reasons for using video in a particular way within the application. You may be expected to justify the decisions you have made when digitising and manipulating video. It is likely that you will need to gather or create source material which is suitable for your application. You may also need to consider the IPR implications of using material.

Section 1

Using video in multimedia applications

In this section we outline the reasons why video is used in multimedia applications and the different effects that video might be used to achieve.

CRUCIAL CONCEPTS

Video can be an impressive element in a multimedia application. Video may form part of the **content** of our application, it may form part of the **interface**, or it may simply be **incidental** for aesthetic reasons. Video is the medium which places the highest demands in terms of storage, bandwidth and processing power.

Video can be the most impressive feature of a multimedia application and it is likely to be the key medium in the next generation of applications. A moving image can convey information much more powerfully than, say, a still image with sound, and certain types of information can only really be communicated in video form. This is particularly true if we want to convey information about dynamic events in the real world, for example a volcano erupting. While we can convey important information about how a volcano is formed using animation and audio narration, or what one looks like using an image, or a text describing what happens during an eruption, only a video can really convey what an erupting volcano is actually like.

However, video is also the most testing media to include, due to the demands it places on the delivery platform in terms of storage, processing and data transfer rates. As a result of this, we must carefully consider the way we use video in our multimedia application. Often we will need to make a compromise between what we would ideally like and what is actually practical. We may, for example, replace a video sequence by a sequence of still images with narration.

Video production is a highly skilled and technically demanding process that includes scripting, direction, lighting, sound recording and so on. It must also be considered in the multimedia design process, for instance by planning it using a storyboard. Video production raises a number of project management questions:

- Will it be necessary to employ consultant video professionals?
- Will lower in-house production values be sufficient?
- Can existing video be reused?

Video can be classified according to the way it is used within a multimedia application – content video, interface video and incidental video.

Content video communicates the content of the multimedia application to the user. It can be used in a variety of situations:

- **Narration** – video is used to present the subject matter. The talent (actor) used for the narration is not important, aside from the fact that they must be able to act, or may need to have a certain accent, or be a specific age, or a have specific look if the application requires it.
- **Testimonials** – a video of a specific person or an historical event. The difference between a narration and a testimonial is that in a narration the person delivers the content, in a testimonial they are the content.
- **Visualisation** – video can be used to show the visual layout and organisation of real world objects, such as building interiors.
- **Processes** – video is particularly well suited to showing processes which take a number of steps or events which occur over time.
- **Reinforcement** – video can be used to complement or add emphasis to the content provided in another medium.

Interface video is part of the interface, such as instructions, rather than being part of the content:

- **Interface instructions** – can be used to explain how to use an application's interface, providing clear instructions about the features.
- **Instructions** – can also be used to explain how to use an application as part of a larger activity, for instance as part of a training course.

Incidental video does not directly inform the user about the content or the interface, but can be used to make the presentation more aesthetically pleasing:

- **Scene setting** – video can be used to establish the scene for the application. This is likely to be appropriate in games, but also in training and educational applications.
- **Transitions** – can be included to provide smooth movement between different sections in an application. This can be particularly effective in games where video transitions are used to join together the different game scenarios.
- **Titles and credits** – are easily created and can add a professional look to an application.
- **Welcome messages** – can be included to add a personal touch to an application.

Quick test

1. What are the three main uses for video within a multimedia application?
2. For each of the main uses of video, what are the typical situations in which they might be used?

Section 2

Desktop video

In this section we look at desktop video and the process of digitising analogue video so that it can be manipulated and delivered in multimedia applications.

───────────────── CRUCIAL CONCEPTS ─────────────────

Desktop video is a digitised representation of an analogue video. When digitising we must choose parameter values for the **frame size**, **colour depth** and **frame rate** in addition to the values for the audio component. Selecting the different values for these parameters has a big influence on the size of the digitised video file.

Using video in multimedia applications typically involves the capture of analogue video, for example from a VCR or a video camera, and conversion into digital form. Some modern video cameras provide digital output directly, so we do not have to digitise.

Analogue video (such as that on a VHS tape) consists of three components: a time code used for synchronisation and editing, a continuous audio track and a series of individual image fields. Because of the way a television picture is displayed, a single picture or frame is composed of two interlaced fields, one of which contains the even rows of the image and one of which contains the odd rows.

Digitisation involves digitising the sound (see Chapter 10) and creating a single digital frame from each pair of fields. Typically this capture and digitisation needs to be supported by hardware.

The audio component has the same features as Digital Audio. When digitising we are faced with the same choices as we are when digitising audio alone: sampling rate, sample depth and the number of channels (mono or stereo).

The choices we have in terms of the image component are similar to those with any bitmapped image (see Chapter 8):

- **Frame size** – the size of a frame in pixels. Your choice of frame size will be restricted by the video capture card and the editing software you use. The typical largest size is 640480.

- **Colour depth** – the colour depth at each pixel. Again the degree of control you have over this will depend on the tools you use. Typical colour depths are the same as with still images, 8-bit, 16-bit and 24-bit (16,777,216 values).

The perception of smooth movement in a video depends critically on how many frames are displayed per second.

- **Frame rate** – the number of frames displayed per second. Your video tools will generally offer you a range of frame rates to choose from.

The frame rate equivalent to a normal television is 25 **fps (frames per second)** which gives a very smooth picture. However, for reasons we will consider in a moment, we are unlikely to use such a high frame rate for our desktop video. We can generally drop the frame rate to 15 fps without making the movement too jerky. If our video doesn't contain any quick movement, we may be able to drop the frame rate to 10 fps.

CRUCIAL TIP

Finding the correct frame rate for a given video clip is an inexact science. You will need to experiment with different frame rates to find the lowest acceptable rate for each clip.

By changing these parameters we can vary the both the quality of the video and the amount of data required to represent it. As we have already said, video will place severe demands on the capabilities of current hardware and software.

The size of a digitised video clip (including audio) in bytes is given by:

file size = duration of recording in seconds × [(frame rate × (colour depth ÷ 8) × frame size) + (audio sample rate × (audio sample depth in bits ÷ 8) × number of audio channels)].

Suppose we wanted to include desktop video in our application and provide close to television quality:

Frame rate: 25 fps
Colour depth: 24-bit
Frame size: 640 x 480 pixels
Audio properties: 44 kHz, 16-bit, stereo

We can calculate the file size for a one second video clip (with audio):

1 × [(25 × (24 ÷8) × (640 × 480)) + (44,100 × (16 ÷ 8) x 2)] = 23,216,400 bytes.

A total of approximately 23Mb – and remember this was a one second clip. Not only is there the issue of storing this quantity of data, there is also the issue of transferring it. The raw data transfer rate of a 40x CD-ROM is around 6Mb per second (though in practice it will be far less than this). Clearly in raw, uncompressed form, the data transfer requirements are simply too great. With very high rate compression we can reduce the file size enough to make it transferable, but we are still likely to **drop frames**. This occurs when the frames making up a video cannot be transferred or converted (compressed or decompressed) quickly enough. Frames are missed out (dropped) making the video jerky. The issue of storing the data is also likely to make it impracticable. Given current technology we need to compromise quality in order to reduce file sizes for our desktop video.

Quick test

1. What are frame rate, frame size and colour depth?

2. What frame rate are we likely to use for a multimedia application?

3. What is the formula for calculating the size of a video file?

Section 3

Video software

In this section we will be considering what general facilities video capture and editing software should possess. When you start using such software it is useful to understand the terminology introduced in the previous section. You should know what basic functionality can be expected from video capture and editing software.

Facilities for capturing video will generally be combined with those for editing it within a single software tool. Digital video can be edited and manipulated in a number of ways, depending on the sophistication of the software used. Typical operations include:

• capturing video and audio from recorded sources via a VCR or directly from a camera	• transitions – inserting transformation between clips, such as dissolves, wipes and zooms
• selecting frame rate, frame size and colour depth and audio settings for capture	• resampling or downsampling – reducing the frame rate, frame size and colour depth to reduce file size
• file format conversion – converting video files from one file format to another	• transparency – superimposing clips, and using mattes
• trimming – removing unwanted portions of the clip	• special effects – applying a variety of image processing filters to clips or individual frames
• cutting and pasting – selecting clips and combining them to form new clips	• changing the time dimension – reversing the clip, making it faster or slower
• simple sound editing – modifying the existing audio and adding new audio	• previewing – viewing the edited clips during the editing process
• adding and animating graphics	• animating clips – moving clips within the video frame
• exporting – writing out an edited clip as a particular file type, with a particular codec, and for a particular data transfer rate.	• adding titles – often these can be animated, for instance to create scrolling titles.

Whilst capturing and editing video it is recommended that you use the same frame rate and frame size as you will use for your final exported video clip. The colour depth should ideally be kept at 24-bit, but if it has to be reduced it is best to do this after the editing has been performed. Some software and **codecs (compression/decompression scheme)** will allow you to generate a custom palette for a clip.

It can also be useful to preserve a high quality archive copy of your digitised video files for future development work, along with the original source material.

Codecs can be compared along a number of different dimensions:

- **Speed of compression and decompression.** A **symmetrical codec** requires the same amount of time to compress and decompress a clip. An **asymmetrical codec** takes significantly different amounts of time for compression and decompression, with compression taking the longest time.

- **Compression ratio.** Different codecs offer different compression ratios and each codec will typically offer a range of ratios.

- **How widely used they are.** If decompression is software based then we can bundle the codec with the application or give the user the opportunity to download it.

- **Quality of the decompressed video.** In a **lossy compression** the decompressed video is not identical to the original, as data has been discarded during the compression process. A **lossless compression** preserves all the data in the original, but generally achieves less good compression ratios. Essentially we have a compromise to make between quality and compression ratio. For most applications we will use a lossy compression for practical reasons, but select a compression ratio that preserves an acceptable level of quality for the user.

- **Whether compression and decompression are hardware or software based.** Compression is typically hardware based and decompression is typically software based. However, better compression ratios and speed of decompression can be achieved when decompression is hardware based.

Quick test

1. What types of operation would a typical video capture and editing software package provide?
2. What is the difference between a symmetrical codec and an asymmetrical codec?
3. What is the difference between a lossy compression and a lossless compression?

Section 4

Gathering video assets

In this section we briefly identify possible sources of video material that can be used in a multimedia application.

There are a number of different ways of acquiring or creating source video for your multimedia application:

- **Create it** – storyboard, script, act and record your own video. You need to be aware that there are restrictions on recording in some locations, also you need to obtain permission and release forms from any actors you use.

- **Commission it** – employ scriptwriters, directors, actors and similar talent to create, perform and record your video. It is important to secure the appropriate intellectual property rights on such recordings.

- **Video clip CD-ROMs** – CD-ROMs containing collections of royalty free video clips which can be incorporated into your multimedia application. You need to be aware that licensing conditions may restrict the way in which these clips can be used, for instance whether they can be edited, whether you need to credit the source, how many you can use within a single application, or how many copies of the application you are allowed to make.

- **World Wide Web video clip collections** – you can download 'copyright free' clips from Web sites. You should be very cautious when using clips from such sites as it can be hard to verify that they actually are copyright free.
- **Film libraries** – libraries that specialise in film may be able to provide you with the clips you require. It is important to be aware of any restrictions on the way the clips can be used and there will typically be a cost involved. You are also unlikely to have exclusive use of the clip.
- **Other video sources** – whilst it can be tempting to record clips from sources such as DVDs, and video cassettes, these are very likely to be protected by copyright.

When creating video it is important to preserve quality. Quality can be affected by a variety of factors including the type of camera and film you use, the microphone, lighting and so on. The process of professional quality video production and recording requires specialist skills and equipment. As a result of this, it may be contracted out to an external company. There are however some steps we can take when producing our own video footage that will improve the subsequent digitised video:

- **Plan.** Use storyboards to plan exactly what you need to shoot. Make sure you have a script (if required) and that your actors are familiar with it. Scout out a good location and check that you don't need permission to film there.
- **Keep scenes short.** Bear in mind that you are not going to be able to include much video in your application.
- **Think about frame size.** Remember your scene will not be shown at the local multiplex, it will be shown on a small area of a computer screen. Long shots are unlikely to be effective.
- **Equipment.** Make sure you have the best and most appropriate equipment for the job. Remember that good lighting can make a lot of difference.
- **Use a tripod.** Keep the camera as steady as possible when shooting your scenes.
- **Use the plan.** Don't shoot footage that you don't need, it wastes time and tape.
- **Keep records.** Keep a record of what scenes are on each tape and where each scene starts and stops. This makes it much easier to locate the scene that you want to digitise.
- **Avoid zooming and panning.** Neither of these digitises well.
- **Consider backgrounds.** An unchanging, simple background will digitise and compress well.

A number of video file formats and codecs are in use and there are software packages for conversion from one format to another.

One possibility we may consider, especially if our application will be delivered over a network, is **streaming video**. In non-streaming video the whole video file must be downloaded before the video can be played. Streaming video plays the video as it arrives. This reduces waiting times and also means that the entire video file is never stored on the user's machine. Streaming video typically requires special server software.

Quick test

1. What are the different ways you might acquire source video for your multimedia application?

2. What steps can we take to improve the creation of our own video footage?

Section 5

End of chapter assessment

Multiple choice questions

1. Which of the following are not uses of content video?

   a) showing processes
   b) narrations
   c) transitions
   d) visualisations
   e) instructions.

2. A one minute video clip (without audio) is captured at a frame size of 320 by 240, a frame rate of 15 fps and a 24-bit colour depth. The size of the resulting file in bytes is –

   a) 3456000
   b) 13824000
   c) 69120000
   d) 207360000
   e) 1658880000.

3. When considering video compression which of the following statements is true?

   a) Lossy compression generally produces lower compression ratios than lossless compression.
   b) Users often cannot see the difference between lossy and lossless compression.
   c) The quality of lossy compression is generally higher than that of a lossless compression.
   d) Lossy compression generally uses a lower frame rate than lossless compression.

Multiple choice answers

1. c) is a use of incidental video. e) is a use of interface video.

2. d) is the right answer. If you calculated a) remember to convert to seconds. If you calculated b) remember to multiply by the fps. If you calculated c) remember to multiply by the colour depth. If you calculated e) remember to divide by 8 to give bytes.

3. b) is true.

Questions

1. You are project manager for a multimedia development project involving the creation of a promotional CD-ROM for a local football club. The CD will be distributed to potential corporate sponsors who will hopefully make use of the corporate hospitality services offered by the club on match days. The clients are keen to use video in the application and have asked that the following video clips be included:

   • a welcome message from the Chairman;
   • a guide to what is on the CD;
   • a tour of the corporate facilities;
   • a tour of the ground;
   • interviews with the star players;
   • historic highlights of the club's success over the years;

- a player's-eye view of walking from the changing rooms onto the pitch on match day with a capacity crowd;
- endorsements from existing corporate sponsors;
- a fly-by of the model showing the proposed redevelopment of the stadium.

As project manager you are concerned that it may not be possible to include all the video clips that the clients have asked for. For each of the clients' proposed clips, formulate your response to the clients, suggesting alternative solutions where appropriate.

2. When converting analogue audio into Digital Audio, the multimedia developer must consider a number of parameters, such as sampling rate and sample depth. The developer has similar parameters to consider when converting analogue video to digital video. Identify these parameters and give examples of typical or recommended parameter values.

3. You are the project manager for a small multimedia development team. Your team does not have a video specialist, so you have delegated the video production work to the authoring programmer. The programmer knows how to operate the camera and how to digitise and edit the film. However, the programmer is unsure how best to approach the creation of the footage and has asked you for advice. Outline the process that should be followed and give tips on producing good source material.

Answers

1. We are being asked to *formulate a response* to the clients' requests for video clips and *suggest alternatives* where appropriate. The overall response is that this is simply likely to be too much video to put on a CD-ROM and would compromise the quality of the application overall. However, the clients have some interesting ideas and we need to consider each of them in turn to see if they should be discarded, implemented in some other media type, or indeed included as video. We must make sure that the suggestions are appropriate to the delivery medium and the purpose of the application. There is no 'right answer' to this type of question, it is more about being able to make sensible judgements and justify them.

- A welcome message from the Chairman. We may want to keep this as a video clip, it adds a nice personal touch to the application and may help to build a personal relationship with the clients. If we were short of storage space, we could replace it with a photograph of the Chairman and an audio welcome message.

- A guide to what is on the CD. This is probably not a good use of video. Text instructions would be more appropriate, we could also include these on the CD packaging.

- A tour of the corporate facilities. We may want to keep this as video as this is key content. An alternative would be a succession of photographs, with text or audio commentary.

- A tour of the ground. It is not clear how important this content is, it can probably be replaced by photographs.

- Interviews with the star players. It is not clear what this adds to the application. If there were good reasons for including it, it may be appropriate to have one very short video interview. Alternatives include photographs and audio or text.

- Historic highlights of the club's success over the years. It may be worth keeping this as video, but going for short edited highlights, rather than trying to include too many. We can present the full list of the club's achievements as text.

- A player's-eye view of walking from the changing rooms onto the pitch on match day with a capacity crowd. This could be a nice way of establishing atmosphere. We could perhaps combine it with the welcome message as the first thing that plays in the application.

- Endorsements from existing corporate sponsors. These would be important, but we need to think carefully about whether they need to be in video form. We would want to preserve their role as testimonials, though again they could be in audio form. Text probably won't carry the same weight.
- A fly-by of the model showing the proposed redevelopment of the stadium. This is likely to be more effective as an animation, possibly providing the user with the ability to control the fly-through. We might also include the architect's drawings.

We are not given any information about the delivery platform, so we cannot be sure that the users will be able to play the video clips. We should ensure that important content is available in other, non-video forms as well. We could suggest that a promotional video tape be produced in addition to the CD-ROM.

2. We are being asked to *identify the parameters used during video digitisation* and *give examples of typical or recommended parameter values*. It is not clear from the question whether we need only consider the parameters relating to the images or whether we need to include the audio as well. We should adopt a cautious approach and include them in case – we are helped by the fact that some of them are listed in the question.

The parameters for the audio component are given in Chapter 10, Section 3:

- sampling rate – typically 44 kHz, 22 kHz or 11 kHz;
- sample depth – typically 8-bit or 16-bit;
- channels – mono (1 channel) or stereo (2 channels).

The parameters for the image component are:

- frame size – typical largest size 640 by 480 pixels;
- colour depth – recommended 24-bit, but could use 16-bit or 8-bit;
- frame rate – typically between 15 and 10 frames per second.

We should provide a context for these parameters – e.g. what does 'frame rate' mean? We should also explain the relationship between quality and file size and make some suggestions as to what parameter values are likely to be reasonable for typical applications.

3. We are being asked to *outline a process for video footage production* and to *give tips on producing source material*. In answering this question we can draw some inspiration from Chapter 3 and consider representing our process in diagram form with an explanatory text. We can also mention some of the legal concerns mentioned in this chapter and Chapter 4. We may also need to make some assumptions – for instance that there is currently a brief written description of the clips that are needed.

There is no predefined process that we need to reproduce in this answer, but we need to outline a sensible and realistic process. We can also weave our tips into our process outline:

i. Agree the duration of each clip with the project team (tip – clips will need to be short).
ii. Produce storyboards for each clip (tip – avoid long shots).
iii. Present storyboards to project team and get feedback.
iv. Write script for each clip.
v. Present scripts to project team and get feedback.
vi. Pick locations (tip – you may need permission to film in some locations, check with legal adviser).
vii. Arrange actors (if required) and props (if required) (tip – make sure actors have time

to learn script. Useful to arrange rehearsals before filming. You will need to get release forms for the actors – check with legal adviser).

viii. Arrange equipment (tip – remember lighting and tripod).

ix. Film each clip (tip – keep a record of what is on each tape, and where each clip is on the tape. Avoid zooming and panning).

x. Check that the footage is satisfactory (tip – it may be worth filming each clip a couple of times and from different angles or with different lighting).

xi. Digitise and edit.

Section 6

Further reading and research

Reading

Jones, F.H. (2002) *How to Do Everything with Digital Video*, McGraw-Hill.
Luther, A.C. (1995) *Using Digital Video*, AP Professional.

Research

Your learning resources centre may have collections of copyright free or licensed video. Find out about these – what conditions are there on their use, what format are they in, how are they categorised? This will be a useful resource when you are developing your applications. You should also look for reputable sources of video on the Web (such as creative.gettyimages.com) as some of these have collections of rights free material. Be sure that the source is reputable as there are many sites which offer media which they claim are copyright free but are in fact not.

Your learning resources centre will have video equipment that you can borrow. Practise with the equipment before you have to use it for an assignment.

Chapter 12
Internet and the World Wide Web

Chapter summary

This chapter provides an introduction to the principles and technologies upon which the Internet and the World Wide Web are based. It also provides just enough to enable you to be able to create basic Web pages using plain HTML.

Learning outcomes

After studying this chapter you should aim to achieve these targets by answering the questions at the end of the chapter. You should be able to:

Outcome 1: Describe the basic workings of the Internet and the Web.
Outcome 2: Develop a basic Web page.
Outcome 3: Evaluate and select appropriate Web authoring tools.

How will you be assessed on this?

In an exam you could be asked to to describe the basic working of the Internet and the Web; write down the HTML that would create a given Web page; discuss the specific issues of Web page design. You might be asked to explain the characteristics of a Web design tool and what advantages/disadvantages they have over a text editor. In course work you might be asked to explain how your Web pages are constructed and what decisions you made.

Section 1

The Internet

In order to develop Web pages effectively it helps to understand the basic workings of the Internet and appreciate some of its limitations.

The **Internet** is a wide area network or WAN that connects and hence allows millions of computers to transfer data between each other. To enable all these computers to communicate with each other requires two important things: a common language of communication or 'protocol' and unique addresses for each computer on the Internet. The protocol the Internet uses is called **TCP/IP**. That stands for transmission control protocol/Internet protocol and defines the way that information from one computer is broken up into bits and relayed to its destination. The TCP/IP protocol enables 'chunks' of data like a file or Web page to be sent to other computers by breaking them up into bits or data packets, adding an address label called a header that includes the sender's address and the recipient's address. TCP/IP then defines how data packets are transmitted across the Internet and then reassembled by the destination computer. Data packets travel around the Internet via 'routers' which are special communication devices which read the header of each data packet and sends it on to the next router (like a post office sorting office) and then finally to the destination address.

Internet or **IP addresses** are 4 bytes long expressed as xxx.xxx.xxx.xxx, e.g. 193.63.150.45 which means there are a total of 2^{32} possible addresses on the Internet. Since it is not easy for humans to remember numbers they can be re-labelled in words so the IP address 193.63.150.45 is also more commonly referred to as www.glam.ac.uk, i.e. its **domain name**. The Internet hosts special computers called **Domain Name Servers** (DNS) which work like telephone directories by maintaining lists that match up an IP address to its corresponding name in words. If, for instance, you enter www.glam.ac.uk into the address bar of your browser and your computer does not already know that www.glam.ac.uk is 193.63.150.45 your computer makes a request to a DNS for the information. If it does not know it tries a different DNS and so on until the required information is found and the request for the selected Web page is made to the appropriate Web server.

The Internet does not do anything of its own accord since it is just a WAN, i.e. a large network of computers. **Internet applications** use the Internet to do something useful like email and the World Wide Web.

CRUCIAL CONCEPTS

The **Internet** is a wide area network that uses the TCP/IP protocol to allow data exchange between computers. Email is an application that uses the Internet.

Internet applications are applications like email that use the Internet to transfer data from one computer to another.

CRUCIAL TIP

You should be able to explain the differences between the World Wide Web and the Internet.

Quick test

What does TCP/IP mean?

Section 2

The Web

As the cost of access drops and the speed of access to the Internet increases the World Wide Web is becoming a major delivery medium for multimedia. To use the World Wide Web for multimedia delivery means you need to understand how it works. This section covers the basic mechanics of the Web and the principles of HTML.

Figure 12.1 illustrates how the Web works. The Web uses its own protocol to transfer data called **HTTP** or Hypertext Transfer Protocol which in turn uses the Internet's protocol TCP/IP (see previous section). The Web uses its own format for data called Hypertext Mark Up Language or **HTML**. **Web browsers** read HTML and try to display it as instructed by the HTML (see below for details on HTML). When a computer or client (Figure 12.1(1)) running a Web browser program like Microsoft's Internet Explorer wishes to display a page of HTML that is located on another computer on the Internet, it needs to make a request to that computer. To do this it sends out an **HTTP Request** (Figure 12.1(2)) for the data. An HTTP request contains information about what data is required and the addresses of the sender and destination. The HTTP request is converted into TCP/IP data packets and sent out across the Internet (Figure 12.1(3)), eventually arriving at the computer with the required information. Only special computers running programs called **HTTP/Web servers** (Figure 12.1(4)) are able to despatch Web files across the Internet. The Web/HTTP server works out what data is required and sends an **HTTP response** (Figure 12.1(5)) over the Internet

(Figure 12.1(3)) which also contains the address of the sender and its destination. When the browser of the requesting computer receives the HTTP response (Figure 12.1(6)) it reads the HTML contained in its data and attempts to display it in the browser window.

HTML is in the form of text; however, Web pages often include many other media types, like images, sounds and videos. To enable HTTP to deal with other media types a set defined types called **MIME-types** have been established. MIME stands for multipurpose mail extensions but they apply to the Web as well as email. Common MIME-types include 'image/jpeg' to denote the data is a JPEG image, 'video/x-msvideo' to denote the data is a Microsoft AVI video file and 'application/x-shockwave-flash' to indicate that the data is a Macromedia Flash file. So an HTTP response might contain many other types of media data other than text. When the browser reads the HTTP response it works out whether it can display the data for each of the MIME-types identified and if it cannot, it will either ignore it or put up a message. So the support of MIME-types allows multimedia Web pages to be constructed. Some MIME-types like the one for Macromedia Flash require a **plug in** or helper program to be able to display them in the browser, and a browser running on a desktop might have several plug ins installed – one for sound file formats, one for video file formats and one for proprietary media types like Flash, etc.

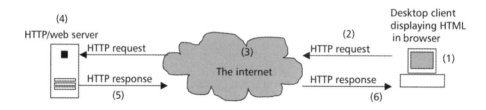

Figure 12.1 How the Web works

CRUCIAL CONCEPTS

HTTP: The protocol used by the Web to enable data to be transmitted between computers on the Internet.
MIME-types: A set of agreed media types recognised by browsers and enabling browsers to display multimedia applications.

Quick test

What does a Web/HTTP server do?

Section 3

Introduction to HTML

In this section you will learn how HTML is constructed and how to use the critical codes to create Web pages. This section only covers the key elements of HTML, for a more detailed coverage of it please refer to one of the reference textbooks at the end of this chapter.

The HTML code that is used to create Web pages is simple ASCII text so any text editor can be used to create it, even tools like Microsoft's Notepad. Figure 12.2 shows a simple HTML document.

```
<html>
    <head>
        <title>
            My first Web page
        </title>
    </head>
    <body>
        <P align="right">This is my first Web page</P>
    </body>
</html>
```

Figure 12.2 A simple HTML document

If you have access to a Windows computer, open up Microsoft Notepad and type in the text from Figure 12.2. Select File and Save and make sure the 'Save as type' option is set to 'All Files (*.*)', type in the File name as 'page1.htm'. Open up Internet Explorer and select File and then Open from the pull down menus and find the file you just saved in Notepad. If you have done this right you should see a white page with some words aligned right and the title of the window should be 'My first Web page'.

HTML is made up of **tags** and **attributes**. A tag starts with the less than sign '<' and end with the greater than sign '>' so browsers knows it is a tag and not just text to be displayed. Attributes and their values modify the tag so the 'align' attribute in the <p> tag in Figure 12.2 tells the browser where to put the text. Tags are often written in upper case and indented, however this is only convention and has no effect on the page displayed. Notice these tags all have what are called 'end tags' indicated by a slash in front of the tag name, e.g. </P> . The beginning and end tags indicate the scope of the tag, i.e. the parts of the document over which it has an effect. When the browser loads up a file of HTML it attempts to interpret what each tag is saying. The example page in Figure 12.2 is straightforward for the browser to interpret but when many tags are used in combination the browser must work harder to interpret and display what is required.

All HTML documents should have these structural tags in this order:

```
<html>
    <head>
        <title>
        :
        </title>
    </head>
    <body>
    :
    :
    </body>
</html>
```

The <html> tag operates over the whole length of the document whereas the <head> tag only operates over a portion of the document. The <html> tag indicates that the following text is all HTML; there are other possible types of Web document but we will not mention them here. The <head></head> tags contain information about the document like its title and key words that describe it. The <body> tag contains the real content of the document. Tags are usually nested within each other so the <title> tag sits within the <head> tag which sits within the <html> tag. The code below is wrong and would result in the title of the page being '</head>' – try making this change with the Web document you have already created and seeing the effect.

```
<html>
<head>
<title>
</head>
</title>
```

It is not possible to explain every HTML tag in this book, for a full consideration see the books noted in the references below. This section will focus on several crucial tags in each of the main tag categories – format, hyperlinking, tables and frames. There are many tags that affect the format of a Web page but the key ones are shown in Figure 12.3.

Tag	Attributes and values	Description
<p>	Align=right/left/center	Paragraph
<b>	None	Bold
<i>	None	Italic
<u>	None	Underline
<h?>	The ? can take values from 1 to 7, e.g. <H4>...</H4>	Predefined headings decreasing in size from 1 to 7
<font>	size=1/2/3/4/5/6/7 color=#?????? Where ?????? is the hexidecimal colour value like #CCFE66 face=a typical font like 'Times Roman'	Makes changes to the font characteristics
<ul>	type=disc/circle/square <li>..</li>needs to be placed before and after each list item	Bulleted list
<ol>	type=A/a/I/i/1 which define the type of number used. <li>..</li>needs to be placed before and after each list item	Numbered list
<img>	src=filename with path or URL, width=width in pixels, height=height in pixels, align=top/bottom/middle/left/right	Inserts an image into a web page

Figure 12.3 Crucial HTML formatting tags

The most important feature of HTML documents is the ability to link from one to another using a **hyperlink**. A basic hyperlink has an anchor which is the item that is clicked, and a destination, the file or document to which the user is taken if the anchor is clicked. Here is a hyperlink in HTML:

```
<a href="docs/details.htm">Click here</a>
```

The anchor is the words 'Click here' and the destination is the file 'details.htm' in the directory 'docs'. The destination file can be located anywhere on the Web and is specified by its **uniform resource locator** or **url** which defines a protocol, the domain name and the path to the destination file. Figure 12.4 contains an example url. The protocol is usually HTTP but could be associated with other Internet applications like ftp (file transfer protocol), gopher, telnet, mailto, etc.

Figure 12.4 Uniform resource locator

The World Wide Web Consortium (http://www.w3c.org), the body responsible for developing and maintaining Web standards, prefer that the term **uniform resource identifier** or **uri** be used rather than uniform resource locator.

The anchor could also be an image:

```
<a href="images/image1.gif"><img src="button3.gif"></a>
```

It is hard with the tags mentioned so far to lay out a Web page as you would wish, e.g. placing a logo in the top right hand corner of the browser window. The <table> tag enables Web designers to lay out pages with more control. Figure 12.5 shows a very simple table with two rows with two cells in each row. The table uses the <tr> tag to create a row and the <td> to create a cell for that row - a row can have as many cells as required. A table cell can contain any other HTML tag including another <table> tag.

```
<table width="50%" border="1">
<tr>
<td>1</td>
<td>2</td>
</tr>
<tr>
<td>3</td>
<td>4</td>
</tr>
</table>
```

| 1 | 2 |
| 3 | 4 |

Figure 12.5 A simple table in HTML, the HTML on the left hand side produces the table on the right hand side

Figure 12.6 shows the HTML used to create the more complex layout shown in Figure 12.7. The table consists of two rows with two cells in the first row and three cells in the second row. The <table> tag has the attributes 'width' which can be specified in pixels or percentage screen width, and 'border' which specifies the thickness of the border in pixels. For layout purposes the border is often set to '0' so that it can not be seen. The <tr> only has the attribute 'align'. The <td> has the attribute 'width' measured in pixels or percentage of the table. Notice that the width attributes in the <td> tags of the first row of the table in Figure 12.6 add up to 100% (36%+64%).

```
<table width="30%" border="1">
<tr>
<td width="36%">These are happy faces:</td>
<td width="64%" align="center">
    <img src="images/happyface.gif" width="72" height="72">
    <img src="images/happyface.gif" width="72" height="72">
</td>
</tr>
<tr>
<td width="36%">This is a sad face:</td>
<td width="64%" align="center">
    <img src="images/sadface.gif" width="72" height="72">
</td>
</tr>
</table>
```

Figure 12.6 A more complex HTML table

159

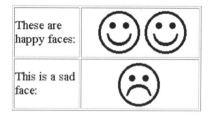

Figure 12.7 The table produced by the HTML code in Figure 12.6

There are two more important attributes of the <td> tag used to help structure tables, 'colspan' and 'rowspan'. Figure 12.8 shows the effect of the colspan attribute on a table, the second cell of the first row has the attribute colspan set to 3 which forces the browser to make the cell with the letter 'b' span the next three cells in following rows.

```
<table width="50%" border="1">
<tr>
<td>a</td>
<td colspan="3">b</td>
</tr>
<tr>
<td>c</td>
<td>d</td>
<td>e</td>
<td>f</td>
</tr>
</table>
```

a	b		
c	d	e	f

Figure 12.8 The effect of the 'colspan' attribute on a table

Figure 12.9 shows the effect of the rowspan attribute on a table, the third cell has the rowspan attribute set to 3 which forces the browser to make the cell with the letter 'b' span the next three rows.

```
<table width="17%" border="1">
<tr>
<td width="35%">a</td>
<td width="65%">c</td>
</tr>
<tr>
<td rowspan="3">b</td>
<td>d</td>
</tr>
<tr>
<td>e</td>
</tr>
<tr>
<td>f</td>
</tr>
</table>
```

a	c
	d
b	e
	f

Figure 12.9 The effect of the 'rowspan' attribute on a table

Another key way of laying out content in a Web page is to use the <frameset> tag. The <frameset> tag enables Web pages to be constructed that include more than one HTML file by breaking up a Web page into sections or 'frames' and then associating each frame with a different HTML file as shown in Figure 12.10.

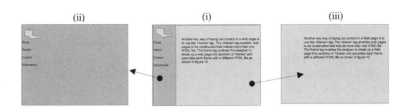

Figure 12.10 The Web page (i) is made up of two other Web pages (ii),
(iii) using the cols attribute

The HTML code below would create the frame arrangement shown in Figure 12.10 and consists of the <frameset> and the <frame> tag where the 'src' attribute in each <frame> tag points to another HTML file. Notice also that this code does not include the <body> tag. The 'cols' attribute defines how large each frame should be, in this instance the first frame takes up 15% and the second 85% of the browser window respectively. The HTML files 'navbar.htm' and 'content.htm' already exist and are normal HTML documents with the <body> tag.

```
<html>
<frameset cols="15%,85%" border="1">
<frame src="navbar.htm" name="leftframe">
<frame src="content.htm" name="mainframe">
</frameset>
</html>
```

Try creating a frameset for yourself. Open up Notepad and create two normal HTML files, one called 'navbar.htm' and the other called 'content.htm' using the same format as shown in Figure 12.2. Create a third file using the code above to create the frameset that 'calls' in these two files, call it 'frame.htm'. Now open a browser window and select File/Open from the pull down menus and navigate and select the file called 'frame.htm'. If you have done this right you will see a Web page similar to that shown in Figure 12.10.

Figure 12.11 shows how we can split up the frame set horizontally instead using the 'rows' attribute. The code to achieve this is shown below.

```
<html>
<frameset rows="15%,85%" border="1">
<frame src="navbar.htm" name="topframe">
<frame src="content.htm" name="mainframe">
</frameset>
</html>
```

Figure 12.11 The Web page (i) is made up of two other Web pages (ii),
(iii) using the rows attribute

Often framesets are used to create navigation bars for Web sites along the top or down the left hand side. For example in Figure 12.10, if a user clicks a hyperlink in the left hand frame named as 'leftframe' the destination file is loaded into the right hand frame named 'mainframe'. This is achieved by adding a new attribute 'target' to the <a> tag which tells the browser where to load, as shown below.

```
<a href="anotherpage.htm" target="mainframe">Details</a>
```

Create a new HTML file in Notepad and call it 'anotherpage.htm', add the HTML code above to the file called 'navbar.htm' and reload the frameset. If you have done this right when you click the link 'Details' in the left hand frame the file called 'anotherpage.htm' should load up in the right hand frame.

There are many other aspects to the <frameset> tag which cannot be covered here. Please refer to the references at the end of this chapter to learn more.

CRUCIAL CONCEPTS

Tags: take the form <*tagname*> and give instructions to the browser on how to display content in a Web page. Most tags have an end tag of the form </*tagname*>.

Attributes: modify a tag and are included within the angle brackets of the tag. Attributes usually have a value e.g. color="#45CDFF".

CRUCIAL TIP

You should be able to create a few simple pages using all the tags outlined in this section, using a text editor so that you can describe the tags in an exam.

Quick test

What are table and frame tags used for in a Web page?

Section 4

Web page design issues

The concepts covered in Chapter 5 and the techniques covered in Chapter 6 address the main issues related to Web page design, as well as multimedia design, and should be applied when designing Web sites and pages. In this section we cover specific Web page design issues.

Web design refers to the specific issues related to creating Web sites and Web pages that contain multimedia elements. When considering the structure of a Web site the key to ensuring that the site is of maximum usability is the design of the site navigation. In general, Web sites should have a home page to which every page in the site is linked. The main navigation menu should be consistent in its appearance, content and position. When navigating down through the site, the relationship between the main menu and submenus should be clear so that users know that a submenu has appeared. Submenus should also obey the same design rules as the main menu.

Screen resolution

The size and screen resolution of PCs varies considerably and designers must compromise between designing to the highest specification PC monitor and ensuring that Web pages appear presentable to the maximum audience. Many users still use PCs with screens of 14/16" with resolutions of 800 by 600 pixels supporting only 256 colours. Many Web design companies design their sites to be acceptable in both 800 by 600 and 1024 by 768 pixel screen resolutions. Alternatively sites can be designed in both page resolutions although this is time consuming and difficult to maintain. Although a particular screen resolution might be 800 by 600, the actual space available in a browser window is 760 by 420 which is the resolution that designers should work to. If it is likely that the Web pages will be printed, designers should work to a width of about 500 pixels to ensure graphics and text print correctly. www.thecounter.com gives some interesting statistics on what browsers, screen resolutions, colour depth, operating systems, etc. are being used.

Design issues

Designers should aim to structure the content of a site so that Web pages have the minimum amount of scrolling. Where scrolling is necessary, the key content should be located near the top. Hyperlinks within the page can also be used to jump up and down the page from a submenu at the top to key sections down the page using bookmarks (see one of the reference books on how to create bookmarks).

Perhaps the key Web design issue is the problem of limited **bandwidth**, that is, the speed of accessing Web pages across the Internet. Web designers must consider very carefully the size in bytes of each page and graphic. Each graphic must be manipulated as indicated in Chapter 8 to minimise its size without reducing the quality of the image. Designers also need to balance the quantity of graphics used to enhance a Web page's appearance and the page's download time. Menus constructed out of graphics could be constructed out of text instead. Delivering multimedia applications over the Web is particularly problematic and is addressed in the next chapter.

There are one or two issues to consider when making decisions about text in a Web page. Since it is difficult to guarantee that users' PCs will have particular fonts installed it is best to use very common fonts to be sure that a Web page is displayed as intended. The common fonts are Arial, Helvetica, Georgia, Courier, Verdana, Times, Times Roman, and Geneva. To increase the chances that the page will be displayed in the way intended multiple fonts can be specified in the 'face' attribute of the <font> tag as shown below:

```
<font face="Verdana, Arial, Helvetica, sans-serif">text</font>
```

It is also possible to specify whether the font should be 'serif' or 'sans-serif' as shown above in case none of the other fonts is installed. Another issue that needs to be taken into account in Web design is the difference in size of fonts displayed on MacIntosh and a PC, i.e. fonts on a PC appear 2 to 3 points bigger than on a MacIntosh and there is no simple solution.

HTML

The **HTML standards** have developed since the early 1990s from version 1, 2, 3.2, 4.0 and now 4.01 (see www.w3c.org for a detailed history) and likewise browsers like Microsoft Internet Explorer have evolved from 2, 3, 4 and now 5. In addition, although Internet Explorer is the dominant browser, a significant minority of other browsers are used. This means that people browsing the Web will be doing so using a variety of different types and versions of browser supporting different versions of HTML. This is very problematic for Web designers who wish their sites to be viewed consistently. The only solution to this is to design to a specific HTML standard like HTML version 4 and stipulate this clearly on the Web site. The disadvantage of this approach is that the designer cannot make use of the most advanced features of the later versions of HTML and browsers. You can check to see if your pages conform to a particular HTML standard by submitting your page to one of the automatic validators, there is one on the www.w3c.org site.

CRUCIAL CONCEPT

Web design: The specific issues of applying multimedia design principles to Web pages.

CRUCIAL TIP

You should be able to explain the concepts and techniques of multimedia design in the context of Web development.

163

Quick test

What considerations do you need to take into account when making decisions about text in a Web page?

Section 5

Web authoring tools

In Section 4 we looked at creating a Web page with a simple text editor. In this section you will study some of the tools that make creating Web pages easier.

HTML editors are the next step up from using a basic text editor to create Web pages. An HTML editor has extra functions built into it, to support the production of HTML code. Figure 12.12 shows an HTML editor called cuteHTML from GlobalScape being used to create an HTML table. cuteHTML includes a colour coding system so that developers can distinguish different classes of tag from each other and from actual content. When you start a new page in cuteHTML it includes the initial structural tags. The other key feature of an HTML editor is the ability to quickly check the appearance of HTML code in a browser window.

```
 1  <HTML>
 2  <HEAD>
 3  <TITLE></TITLE>
 4  <META name="description" content="">
 5  <META name="keywords" content="">
 6  <META name="generator" content="CuteHTML">
 7  </HEAD>
 8  <BODY BGCOLOR="#FFFFFF" TEXT="#000000" LINK="#0000FF" VLINK="#800080">
 9
10  <table border="1" width="100%">
11  <tr>
12  <t
13  <t  ■ table          b</td>
14  </ ■ td
15  <t  ■ textarea
16  <t  ■ th
17  <t  ■ title
18  </ ■ tr
19  </ ■ tt
20  </HTML>
21
```

Figure 12.12 cuteHTML being used to construct a table in HTML

The next class of tools up from HTML editors are full **Web page design tools**. There are several available including Macromedia Dreamweaver, Adobe GoLive and Microsoft Frontpage. Web design tools allow you to see what a Web page looks like as it is being developed. All these tools share these common features:

- ability to see pages as they are being developed – WYSIWYG;
- easy switching between editing source HTML code and the WYSIWYG editor;
- many wizards for speeding up the development process like creating the navigation bar or formatting text;
- ability to insert and manipulate tables, hyperlinks and frame tags easily;
- ability to insert other multimedia objects like images, sound, videos;
- set up template to standardise the appearance of pages for a whole site;
- preview pages in different browsers;
- adjust the attributes of any tag using dialogue boxes;
- site management.

Figure 12.13 shows Macromedia Dreamweaver MX being used to create a table. Developers can edit the page either in HTML code, in the WYSIWYG view or switch between the two. Figure 12.13 shows the 'Property browser' for the current table cell (</td>) which allows the developer to change its attributes like width, background colour, alignment, etc.

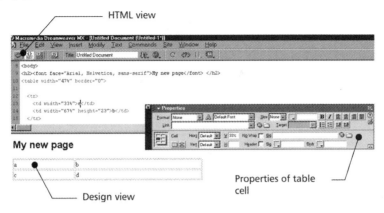

Figure 12.13 Macromedia Dreamweaver MX being used to develop a table

The big advantage of using a Web design tool is the ability to see and manipulate page designs easily. The disadvantage is that the design view is not completely the same as the view seen in a browser because the browser itself decides how best to display the page. The disadvantage of using Web design tools is the loss of control over the HTML code generated and the increased difficulty of ensuring the Web pages comply with particular HTML standards.

─────── CRUCIAL CONCEPTS ───────

HTML editor: A specialist text editor which supports HTML tags, provides an ability to format HTML and preview pages in browsers.

Web page design tool: A WYSIWYG tool for creating Web pages that has many features and wizards for supporting Web page design.

Quick test

What are the main features of a Web page design tool?

End of chapter assessment

Multiple choice questions

1. Which of the following statements are true of the Internet?

   a) the Internet is a large local area network
   b) the basic protocol of the Internet is FTP
   c) domain Name Servers allocate IP numbers
   d) the Web is an Internet application.

2. Which of the following statements are true of the Web?

   a) the Web and the Internet are the same
   b) web browsers send out HTTP responses
   c) different media are defined by their MIME-type
   d) web pages are constructed in HTTP.

3. What is the correct HTML code to produce the following effect?

A happy birthday to you

   a) `<b>A happ</b><font color="gray ">y birth</font><i>day to</i><u>you</u>`
   b) `<b>A happ</b>y<font color="gray "> birth</font>day to<i><u>you</u>`
   c) `<b>A happy</b><font color="gray "> birth</font><i>day </i>to<u>you</u>`
   d) `<b>A happ</b>y<font color="gray "> birth</font><i>day to</i><u>you</u>`

4. What is the correct HTML code to turn the image 'image1.gif' into a hyperlink to 'file1.htm'?

   a) `<img href="image1.gif"><a src="file1.htm">link</a>`
   b) `<img src="image1.gif"><a href="file1.htm">link</a>`
   c) `<a href="file1.htm"><img src="image1.gif"></a>`
   d) `<a src="file1.htm"><img href="image1.gif"></a>`
   e) `<a href='image1.gif'><img src='file1.htm'></a>`

5. What is the missing tag in the following HTML document?

```
<HTML>
    <HEAD>
        <TITLE>
        </TITLE>
    <BODY>
        <h1>HELLO</H1>
        <IMG SRC="image1.gif">
        </BODY>
    </HTML>
```

   a) `</HEAD>`
   b) `<HEAD>`
   c) `<B>`
   d `<META>`
   e) `</BODY>`

6. The following HTML code represents a layout of a page. Which of the options, shown on the next page, does it represent?

```
<table border="1" width="50%">
<tr>
<td rowspan="2" width="20%"><img src="qmresources/happyface.gif" width="72"
height="72"></td>
<td colspan="2" align="center">
<h2>The Title of this page</h2>
</td>
</tr>
<tr>
<td bgcolor="gray">  : </td>
</tr>
</table>
```

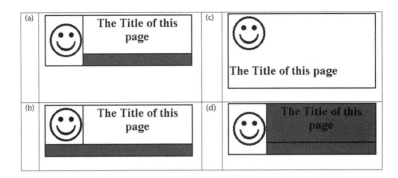

7. What is the correct code to create the following frame arrangement?

| (a) | ```
<frameset cols="10%,90%" frameborder="YES" >
   <frame name="leftFrame" src="blank.htm">
   <frameset rows="10%,90%">
      <frame name="subnavigation" src="blank.htm">
      <frame src="blank.htm" name="Content">
   </frameset>
</frameset>
``` | (c) | ```
<frameset rows="10%,90%" frameborder="YES">
   <frame name="topFrame" src="blank.htm" >
   <frameset cols="10%,90%" >
      <frame name="leftFrame" src="blank.htm">
      <frame name="content" src="blank.htm">
   </frameset>
</frameset>
``` |
|---|---|---|---|
| (b) | ```
<frameset cols="10%,90%" frameborder="YES" >
   <frame name="leftFrame" src="blank.htm">
   <frame src="blank.htm" name="Content">
   <frame src="blank.htm" name="subnavigation">
</frameset>
``` | (d) | ```
<frameset rows="10%,90%" frameborder="YES">
   <frameset cols="10%,90%" >
   </frameset>
</frameset>
``` |

8. Which of the following statements are true of Web page design?

   a) you should always design to a resolution of 1024 by 768
   b) most home computers use 17" monitors
   c) web designers should use standard fonts
   d) pages designed in HTML version 4 will work properly in every browser version.

9. Which of the following statements are true of Web authoring tools?

   a) the advantage of an HTML editor is that you can see the page design
   b) the design view and browser view of a Web page in a Web page design tool are not exactly the same
   c) the disadvantage of Web page design tools is that you can only see one view of a page at a time
   d) you cannot edit the HTML in Web page design tools.

Multiple choice answers

1. d)
2. c)
3. c)
4. c)
5. a)
6. a)
7. a)
8. c)
9. b)

Questions

1. Explain how one computer on the Internet communicates with another computer on the Internet.

2. Explain what happens when someone using a Web browser clicks on a hyperlink.

3. How would you use the <table> tag to create the home page for an online magazine? What is the difference between the <table> tag and the <frameset> tag?

4. How can the principles of multimedia design be applied to Web page design? What are the specific issues of Web page design?

5. What tools do you use to create Web pages? If you were selecting a Web page design tool what features would you be looking for?

Answers

1. Your answer should start by explaining what the Internet is – a large wide area network using TCP/IP as its underlying protocol. You should then explain how TCP/IP works and then explain how IP numbers enable each computer on the Internet to be uniquely identified so that data from one computer can be sent safely to another. You need to explain how domain names are used instead of IP numbers and how domain name servers are used for this purpose.

2. This question is asking you to explain what you know about the workings of the Web. You could start by explaining the differences between the Internet and the Web: the Web is an application that uses the Internet and the Internet is simply the underlying network. Once you have explained this you can, with the aid of a diagram, explain how HTTP works. Next you can explain how hyperlinks are constructed in HTML and their associated url – uniform resource locator. The url tells the browser precisely where the file in the hyperlink can be found. You can then explain how the browser attempts to obtain the file using HTTP.

3. The first part of this question is asking for two things: how the tag works and how it would be used in creating a home page for an online magazine. Start by explaining that the table tag is made up of the <tr> table row, and the <td> table cell and the actual content is contained within the <td></td> tags. Explain that a table is constructed of rows and each row contains a number of cells which defines the number of columns in the table. A good answer would also explain how the width, colspan and rowspan attributes modify the table design. Finally explain that the table tag is used primarily to arrange the layout of content in a Web page by setting the border attribute to zero.

   For the online magazine you could draw the layout of its homepage that included a main navigation menu, space for its logo, content area and perhaps submenu. When you have done this you can explain how a table tag would be used to construct it.

4. To answer the first part of this question you need to refer back to Chapters 5 and 6. For the second part of the question you need to discuss a range of issues:

- the design of the site navigation;
- the size and resolution of the screen;
- designing for limited bandwidth;
- limiting the use of fonts;
- designing to specific versions of HTML.

5. Your answer should start by explaining that there is a range of tools available for creating Web pages, from simple text editors to WYSIWYG Web page design tools. Then explain the functionality of HTML editors:

- auto insertion of HTML tags and attributes;
- colour coding of HTML, e.g. tags in blue, content in black;
- quick preview of HTML in browser.

Web page design tools allow you to see Web pages as they are being designed although these will not be quite the same as the way they appear in a browser.

Good answers will also mention image editing tools like Adobe Photoshop and Macromedia Fireworks which allow you to optimise images for Web delivery. Good answers might also mention other multimedia tools like video editing tools such as Adobe Premiere, animation tools like Macromedia Director and sound editing tools like Sonix SoundForge.

In the second half of the question you should note that good Web page design tools should include the following features:

- page design and HTML view of document;
- wizards for speeding up development;
- wizards for inserting and manipulating tables, hyperlinks and frames;
- ability to insert other multimedia objects like images, sound and video;
- templates for standardising page design;
- site management facilities.

Section 7

Further reading

Reading

Castro, E. (1999) *HTML 4 for the World Wide Web, 4th Edition, Visual QuickStart Guide*, Peach Pit Press.

Musciano, C. and Kennedy, B. (2002) *HTML & XHTML: The Definitive Guide, 5th Edition*, O'Reilly & Associates, Inc.

Chapter 13
Advanced applications

Chapter summary

This chapter provides an introduction to some of the more advanced techniques in Web page development and also an overview of future developments in the area of multimedia technologies.

Learning outcomes

After studying this chapter you should aim to achieve these targets by answering the questions at and the end of the chapter. You should be able to:

Outcome 1: Apply simple styles to a Web page.
Outcome 2: Determine how to enhance Web pages with dynamic HTML.
Outcome 3: Insert multimedia elements into a Web page.
Outcome 4: Describe new multimedia technologies.

How will you be assessed on this?

In an exam you could be asked to demonstrate the use of styles to improve the appearance of a Web page; explain how Web pages can be made dynamic with the aid of scripting and addition of multimedia elements. You could be asked to outline advances in multimedia technology and their importance. In course work you would be expected to explain how you have applied styles, scripting and multimedia to your Web pages. You might be asked to write an essay on the future of multimedia.

Section 1

Cascading Style Sheets

In the last chapter you learnt how to create Web pages that included formatted text, images, hyperlinks, tables and frames. In this section we look at how you can improve the look of your Web pages with styles.

The formatting of Web page content is very limited in standard HTML so a new feature was added to HTML version 4 called **Cascading Style Sheets** (CSS). CSS enable styles and formats of Web page elements to be defined separately from the content of the page. Figure 13.1 shows how a style is defined to format all paragraphs, i.e. <p> tags in a Web page. Styles are placed in the <head> tag so that the style can apply to all <p> tags in the Web page. This approach of including the styles in the <head> tag is called **embedded style sheets**. The advantage of this is that to change the appearance of all paragraphs in a Web page only requires changing the style once in the <head>tag. Figure 13.1 includes a **style rule** to format all paragraphs with Arial, 14 point size font. A style rule consists of at least one property, e.g. 'text-decoration' and a corresponding value, e.g. 'underline' with each style rule separated by a semicolon. There is another type of style rule defined in

Figure 13.1 called a **style class**. Class declarations are preceded by a period and only apply to elements that specify that class as shown in the second paragraph tag in Figure 13.1. Figure 13.2 shows what this HTML looks like in a browser; notice that the second paragraph inherits the paragraph style rule but has the italic text decoration added. Try typing the code in Figure 13.1 into a text editor and saving as a Web document with the name 'css.htm', then load the file into a browser using the File/Open pull down options.

```
<html>
     <head>
          <style>
               p      {font-size:14 pt;font-family:arial,sans-serif;}
               .upara {text-decoration: underline; background-color: #cccccc;}
          </style>
     </head>
<body>
     </p> A paragraph formatted with a style</p>
     <p class="upara">A paragraph formatted with a style class</p>
</body>
</html>
```

Figure 13.1 HTML containing a style declaration in the <head> tag

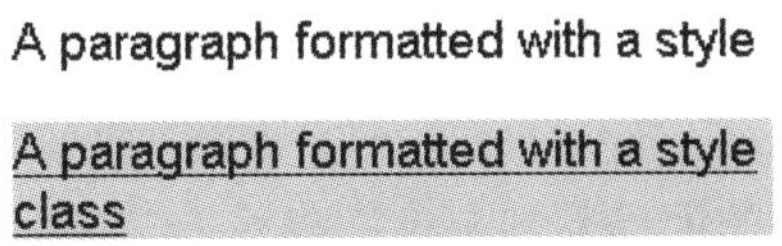

A paragraph formatted with a style

A paragraph formatted with a style class

Figure 13.2 Web page produced from the code in Figure 13.1

There are very many styles available for designers to use to improve the appearance of their Web pages and it is impossible to mention them all here. Figure 13.3 contains details of some the most commonly used styles . A good Web site to find out more about styles is at www.w3schools.com/ or see the references at the end of this chapter.

Font properties	
Property name	Values
font-family	*fontname*
font-style	italic, oblique
font-weight	normal, bold, lighter – a value between 100 and 900
font-size	a value in points or pixels e.g. 12pt or 12px
Text Properties	
vertical-align	sub, super, top, middle, bottom – a percentage value e.g. 45%
line-height	a value in points or pixels e.g. 10pt or 10px
text-alignment	left, right, center, justify
List properties	
list-style-type	disc, square, decimal
list-style-image	url to image location
Margin and border properties	
margin	value in points or pixels, e.g. 20pt or 20px
border-style	dotted, dashed, solid, double, groove, ridge
border-width	value in points or pixels, e.g. 10pt or 20px
Color and background properties	
background-color	value in hexidecimal, e.g. #33FF00
background-image	url to image location

Figure 13.3 Commonly used styles

CSS-positioning is another important feature introduced with HTML 4 which makes it possible to define the height, width, visibility and position of a style class. CSS-positioning allows you to position content anywhere in a Web page without using the <table> tag, as shown in Figure 13.4. The code in Figure 13.4 includes the definition of a style called 'layer1' with its position, size and visibility; notice that the style is preceded by a hash ('#') not a period. To use the new style we need to insert a <span> tag into the body of the document with a reference the new style 'id=layer1'. Most HTML tags can be included between the <span> tags. If any other <span> tag references the layer1 style class they will also be placed in the same position so care should be taken.

```
<html>
    <head>
    <style>
        #layer1 {position:absolute; top:100px; left:200px; height:80px;
            width: 200px; visibility: visible;}
    </style>
    </head>
    <body>
    <span id="layer1"> I'm here</span>
    </body>
</html>
```

<p align="center">Figure 13.4 Specifying size and position of a style class</p>

CSS and CSS-P require browsers that support HTML 4. However unfortunately the implementation of HTML 4 differs between Netscape's browsers and Microsoft's browsers, making it difficult to ensure that your Web pages will look right in either.

CRUCIAL CONCEPTS

Cascading style sheets: A feature added to HTML 4 that gives designers more control over the appearance of a Web page by specifying style rules for Web page elements.
CSS-positioning: Allows the position, size and visibility of a style class to be specified.

Quick test

How can cascading styles improve the appearance of a Web page?

Section 2

Web page scripting

In this section we introduce you to the principles of Web page scripting. A complete coverage of scripting is beyond the scope of this book; if you want to know more please refer to one of the books in the reference section of this chapter or go to www.w3schools.com/ for tutorials in Web page scripting. The intention of this section is to give you a brief overview of how scripting works and is used in Web pages to create dynamic HTML.

Standard HTML pages are static, i.e. when a page is loaded into a browser it remains the same, however long the page is displayed and whatever the user does. **Web page scripting** can make your Web pages dynamic by adding animation and interactivity. Web page scripting simply means adding programming code to your Web pages. It is called scripting rather than programming because the code is retained as text and is not compiled. There are two main scripting languages used in Web pages, **Javascript** and **VBscript,** although Javascript is by far the most popular. Javascript has all the expected features of a programming language and is used in the examples given in this chapter.

Figure 13.5 shows the simplest way of including scripting in Web page. This code causes a message box saying 'Welcome' to be displayed when users move their mouse over the image. This code contains two key elements of scripting, **events** and **functions**. To make Web pages responsive to what the users do we need to 'trap' events like clicking the left-hand mouse button, moving the pointer over a page element like an image. The piece of code in Figure 13.5 'onmouseover' traps the event of users moving their pointers over the image 'image1.gif'. Once the event has been trapped the script must then do something with it and that is what functions are for. In Figure 13.5 when the mouseover event is trapped the function 'alert()' is called. The function 'alert()' outputs any message enclosed between the two brackets. Javascript includes many standard functions but you can write your own as well.

```
<img src="image1.gif" onmouseover="alert('Welcome');">
```

Figure 13.5 Javascript scripting included in a Web page

The script in Figure 13.6 shows how you can write your own functions in Javascript and is also a better way of including Javascript in a Web page than embedding it in the tags throughout the page, as shown in Figure 13.5. The Javascript in Figure 13.6 is inserted between the <script></script> tags in the <head> tag. The code in Figure 13.6 causes the image to change when users move their mouse over it. Two functions have been defined 'fover()' and 'fout()', fover() causes the 'src' attribute of the image called 'button1' to be changed to 'image1over.gif' and the second causes it to be changed to 'image1.gif'. The image tag has traps for the two events 'onmouseover' and 'onmouseout' and calls the functions fover() and fout() respectively hence changing the 'src' attribute of the image. Functions that are executed when an event happens are referred to as **event handlers**.

```
<html>
<head>
    <script>
function fover(){
        window.document.button1.src="image1over.gif";
    }

function fout(){
        window.document.button1.src="image1.gif";
    }
    </script>
</head>
<body>
    <img src="image1.gif" height="100" width="100" name="button1"
    onmouseover="fover()" onmouseout="fout()">
</body>
</html>
```

Figure 13.6 Javascript used to create a rollover image in a Web page

You will notice that the line of script in Figure 13.6 that changes the 'src' attribute of the image is:

```
window.document.button1.src="image1.gif"
```

The line of script above refers to the 'src' attribute using something called the **document object model**. The document object model is a means of referencing every object and their attributes in a Web page and is based on a hierarchy as shown in Figure 13.7. Hence the reference to the image 'button1' above is prefixed with 'window.document' although this 'long hand address' is not always entirely necessary and 'button1.src' is sufficient here.

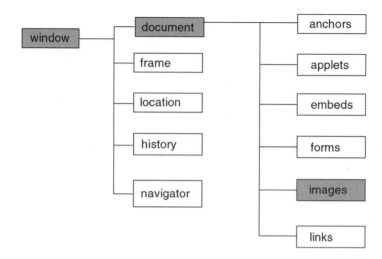

Figure 13.7 The basic document object model indicating the hierarchy to the 'images' object

The previous section showed how Cascading Style Sheets can be used to set the values of many new properties of Web page elements. These new properties can also be set in Javascript and hence extend the document object model shown in Figure 13.7 considerably. For instance, in Figure 13.1 a style called .upara is defined, this could be redefined in Javascript with the following line:

```
document.all.upara.style.text-decoration='none';
```

Likewise the position of the style called #layer1 in Figure 13.4 could be changed with the following lines:

```
document.all.layer1.style.left='500px';
```

Unfortunately Netscape's implementation of the document object model is different from Microsoft's, which means that it is difficult to ensure pages using scripting designed for one browser will work in the other browser. There are also differences between generations of browser.

The combination of HTML, Javascript, cascading style sheets and the document object model is often referred to as **dynamic HTML** or **DHTML**. DHTML allows you to add interactivity and animation to a Web page. Web page design tools like Dreamweaver include many features that support the development of DHTML including animation, rollovers and other user interactions.

─────────── CRUCIAL CONCEPTS ───────────

Web page scripting: Executable code in the form of scripts that can be added to Web pages to make them interactive or dynamic.

Document object model: A means of referencing all the elements in a Web page making them accessible to scripts.

Dynamic HTML/DHTML: The combination of HTML, Javascript, Cascading Style Sheets and the document object model.

─────────── CRUCIAL TIP ───────────

Try learning and using the dynamic features of a Web page design tool like Dreamweaver and then, if you have done some programming elsewhere, see if you can understand any of the Javascript code that is generated.

Quick test

In what way do Cascading Style Sheets improve Web page design?

Section 3

Multimedia on the Web

In this section we explain how multimedia elements are added to a Web page and the issues of adding multimedia elements to your Web pages.

We have already seen how to include images into a Web page in Section 3, Chapter 10. However it is possible to include sound, video, animation and interactivity in Web pages as well.

Web browsers on their own cannot handle media like sound and video unless they can call other helper programs called **plug-ins** to handle them. When a browser finds media in an HTML file of a MIME-type it cannot immediately display it looks to see whether it has a plug-in program associated with that MIME-type to handle it. There are very many plug-ins available to handle many different MIME-types and there are many different plug-ins for handling common sound and video formats. The most common plug-ins used for sound and video are:

- Microsoft Windows Media Player;
- RealMedia Real Media Player;
- Apple QuickTime.

One of the main problems of including multimedia elements in a Web page is that you have no control over what plug-ins are being used by your users' browsers. This means that you lose some control over how your Web pages will appear. The best that you can do is advise your users of your Web pages what plug-ins you recommend and include details of how to get the plug-in.

Media can either be embedded into Web pages so that they are in line with the other content of the page or they can run in their own windows. There are several ways of embedding media in a Web page. The easiest way is using the <embed> tag inside the <object> tag as shown below to include a sound file in a Web page.

```
<object>
<embed src="intro.wav" height=60 width=200>
</object>
```

The effect of the above in a Web page is shown in Figure 13.8 using Windows Media Player (remember this would look different if a different plug-in was used).

Figure 13.8 Embedded sound file in a Web page using the Windows Media Player plug-in

It is possible to arrange for the sound file to play automatically and without the control bar by adding two extra attributes as shown here:

```
<object>
<embed src="intro.wav" height="60" width="200" autostart="true" hidden="true">
</object>
```

If you want your media to run in a separate window you can use a normal hyperlink as shown below:

```
<a href="intro.wav">play intro</a>
```

The same approach applies to video files as shown here:

```
<object>
<embed src="intro.avi" height="200" width="200">
</object>
```

Since video and sound files are invariably large and the speed of accessing Web pages is often slow, it is important to try to reduce their size using the appropriate editing tools before embedding them in a Web page. The process of reducing the size of a media file is sometimes called **nibbling** and involves repeatedly reducing the size of a file using editing tools, checking the quality of the media and deciding whether the file can be reduced further in size without affecting its quality. The techniques that can be used to reduce the size of sound files include:

- resample at a lower sampling frequency, e.g. from 44KHz to 22KHz;
- change from stereo to mono;
- increase the compression ratio;
- change the codec;
- use a different file format.

The techniques that can be used to reduce the size of video files include:

- resample at a lower screen resolution typically reducing it to 120 by 240 pixels;
- resample at a lower sampling rate, i.e. from 25 frames per second to 15;
- increase the compression ratio;
- change the codec;
- apply the techniques outlined above for sound if the video includes a sound track;
- use a different file format.

Animation and interaction can be included in Web pages in two ways. You could use DHTML as explained in Section 2 above or you can use proprietary multimedia authoring tools like Macromedia Director and more likely Macromedia Flash. Macromedia Director is a tool for creating interactive multimedia applications for CD-ROM and the Web. Macromedia Flash does likewise but is more specifically aimed at producing applications for Web delivery and was discussed in Chapter 9 on animation. Once you have created an application in Director or Flash you need to prepare it for Web delivery and ensure the appropriate plug-in is installed in the browser. For Director files the plug-in is called the **Shockwave player** and for Flash files the plug-in is called the **Flash player**. Embedding a Shockwaved Director file or Flash file uses the same code that is used to embed sound and audio files as shown below.

```
<object >
<embed src="intro.dcr" width="300" height="300">
</embed>
</object>
```

There are tools built into Director and Flash which optimise this code by adding extra information and attributes for Web delivery.

Embedding sound and video files is acceptable for very small clips of less than 1Mbyte, but files over this size result in much longer download times even for computers with relatively fast Internet connections. Users must wait for the whole file to download before they can see or hear it played. The solution to displaying files larger than 1Mbyte on the Web is to use **streaming** technologies. Streaming involves using special server programs and a different protocol to HTTP called **real time streaming protocol** (RTSP) to send sound and video files across the Internet. Streamed sound and video files begin to play as soon as the first few bytes have been downloaded and are not stored on the destination computer like embedded files. Streamed sound and video usually require a dedicated streaming server separate from the HTTP server. Currently there are three main providers of streaming server software: Microsoft Windows Media Services; Apple Darwin Streaming Server; and RealMedia RealServer, and all three use RTSP and are free for basic installations.

CRUCIAL CONCEPTS

Plug-in: A special helper program to handle MIME-types that the browser cannot. Plug-ins are used to play media files.

Streaming: The technique of playing large media files in a browser as the files are downloading. Streaming requires its own protocol RTSP and its own server.

CRUCIAL TIP

Try embedding a sound or video file into a Web page using the code outlined in this section.

Quick test

Why is the process of 'nibbling' important in preparing media for Web delivery?

Section 4

New technologies

Multimedia technologies are evolving rapidly – streamed video on the Web was not available a decade ago but is now becoming a mature technology. So in this section we review two of the key emerging multimedia technologies which are likely to become important in the decade ahead.

At the moment there is a revolution going on with the **convergence** of three key technologies, computing, telecommunications and television and the blurring of the boundaries between them. This convergence means that you can now get the services and applications available from any one of these three technologies in any of the other two. For example it is now possible to surf the Web on you television, see videos on mobile phones and watch television on your computer. There are two key developing multimedia technologies that stand out as part of this convergence of technologies – mobile phone communications and interactive/digital television.

Current mobile communications technologies are limited to text and sound and have very little interactivity. Most current mobile phones are referred to as 1G – first generation. A new generation of mobile technology is now available which is referred to as 2G or sometimes 2.5G. **2G mobile phones** are based on technologies which are still good for voice communications but provide limited access to the Web in the form of text pages based on a simplified version of HTML called Wireless Mark-up Language or WML. The problem with 2G mobile phones is that they are too slow and limited to text and voice. There is considerable research and development under way world wide to create **3G mobile phones**. 3G mobile phones are being designed to:

- create a global mobile telephone system so that you can use your phone anywhere in the world;
- increase access speeds from 10-20 Kbit/s to 300-400Kbit/s;
- provide a permanent connection to the Internet/ Web;
- provide real time interactive multimedia communications.

3G mobile technologies will mean that existing mobile devices – mobile phones, personal data assistants and music players will merge into one multi-purpose device using a high definition colour screen with good quality speakers or audio output.

There are a number of competing 3G wireless network technologies:

- General Packet Radio Service (GPRS);
- Universal Mobile Telecommunications System (UMTS);
- Code Division Multiple Access 2000 (CDMA2000);
- Enhanced Data rates for Global Evolution (EDGE).

The fact that there are competing technologies means that the objective of a global mobile telephone system will not be achieved in the short term. The sort of multimedia applications that 3G mobile technologies will support include:

- browsing media-rich Web pages;
- real time multimedia communications with friends, family and colleagues;
- media rich shopping;
- network gaming;
- interactive learning.

Interactive television, sometimes referred to as ITV, has become possible because of the advent of **digital television**. Digital television means that the signal is broadcast in a digital format so receiving televisions must be able to decode it before they can display it. Digital television is now available via cable, satellite and even terrestrial broadcasting technologies although most viewers still view their television via analogue transmissions. To view digital television in the UK you need to have a **set top box** which is an additional piece of equipment that looks a bit like a video recorder to decode the digital television signal before displaying it. Or you need an **integrated digital television** (iDTV) which has the decoding equipment built in. In addition a **return path** is required to make a digital television interactive, i.e. to allow viewers to make choices, conduct transactions or navigate through screens of content. Currently the return path for satellite and terrestrial digital television is done via a modem built into the set top box and telephone line. However both satellite and terrestrial broadcasting technologies are being developed to enable the radio signals themselves to carry the return path. For cable digital television the cable is able to carry the return path. There are many standards being developed and used around the world to support digital broadcasting, however the most popular is called **DVB** – digital video broadcasting, which comes in a number of compatible versions: DVB-S for satellite transmissions, DVB-T for terrestrial and DVB-C for cable. DVB uses the MPEG-2 compression standard to compress the video signal before transmission. **High definition television (HDTV)** is another development that greatly improves the quality of the television picture. HDTV requires greater bandwidth than that which will be provided by television broadcasters in the UK (although DVB-T does support HDTV) and means fewer channels can be transmitted. The decision was made in the UK to offer more digital channels rather than better picture quality whereas the opposite decision was made in the United States.

Interactive television provide a range of new kinds of service to views:

- **Video on demand** which means viewers will be able to pay to view films when they want and be able stop, rewind and forward the film as if they had hired it from a video rental shop.

- **Personal video recorders** (PVR) which will be able to record up to 100 hours of broadcast television for each person in the household and will be intelligent enough to anticipate what programs to record and give viewers a menu of recorded programs. PVRs require large amounts of disk storage.
- **Electronic program guides** (EPG) which allow viewers to select/preview channels through a menu system.
- Electronic encyclopaedias.
- Interactive learning.
- Interactive games.
- E-commerce.
- Ability to vote or make choices about the story lines of films and dramas and issues of current affair.

CRUCIAL CONCEPTS

Convergence: The tendency of Internet and Web technologies, mobile communication technologies and television to converge into one technology where the services of each are available through the others.
Interactive television: Enables viewers to make choices, conduct transactions and navigate information whilst watching television.
Personal video recorders: Semi-intelligent digital video recorders that require extremely high capacity disk drives but allow viewers to record up to 100 hours of programmes and select recorded programmes from on screen menus.
Electronic program guides: Sophisticated, navigable and comprehensive on-screen programme guides that are regularly updated.

CRUCIAL TIP

Visit the Web sites of the key players in new technologies like the BBC to find out what are the latest developments in new multimedia technologies.

Quick test

What services do 3G mobile phones offer?

Section 5

End of chapter assessment

Multiple choice questions

1. Which of the following is a correct style rule to format all paragraphs?

   a) `p (font-size;14pt:)`
   b) `p {fontsize: 14pt}`
   c) `p {font-size:14pt;}`
   d) `p {font-size - 14pt;}`

2. Which of the following statements is true of Cascading Style Sheets?

   a) styles can only be included within an individual Web document
   b) CSS-P allows you to format text
   c) a style rule contains a style sheet and corresponding value
   d) a style rule contains at least one style property.

3. Which of the following statements is true?
   a) Web page scripting is another name for HTML
   b) Javascript and VBscript are the same
   c) Javascript can include functions
   d) Javascript can only be included in an HTML tag.

4. Which of the following statements is true?
   a) events are used to trap functions
   b) the value of style properties can be set in Javascript
   c) the value of style properties cannot be set in Javascript
   d) the document object model is the same as DHTML.

5. Which of the following HTML statements is correct?
   a) `<object src="intro.wav>click here</object>`
   b) `<embed height=60 width=200></embed>`
   c) `<embed src="intro.wav></embed>`
   d) `<a embed="intro.wav">click here</a>`

6. When inserting multimedia elements in a Web page –
   a) the browser searches for the correct MIME-type to display it
   b) the size of file should not matter
   c) streaming is used to reduce the file size
   d) resampling is used in the process of 'nibbling'.

7. In mobile communications –
   a) 3G phones will increase access speeds to 10-20Kbit/s
   b) 2G phones will supersede 3G phones
   c) 3G phones aim to create a global telephone system
   d) 2G phones can display media rich Web pages.

8. In interactive television –
   a) digital television requires a set top box
   b) the return path is not important
   c) it is only available via satellite
   d) personal video recorders will be a new service.

Multiple choice answers

1. c)
2. d)
3. c)
4. b)
5. c)
6. d)
7. c)
8. d)

Questions

1. How can a basic Web page that just included text and graphics be enhanced?
2. What are the issues involved in enhancing a Web page with more advanced features?
3. What is DHTML and how can it add interactivity to a Web page?
4. In what ways will multimedia applications be accessed in the future?

Answers

1. The objective of this question is to ascertain how much you know about the mechanics of enhancing a Web page with CSS, DHTML and multimedia. You should explain how CSS could improve the appearance of a Web page and CSS-P allows you to position content more accurately. You should also be able to give an example of how a style is defined in a Web document. Next you should explain what DHTML is and then say how it adds interactivity to a Web page by having event handler functions that trap user interactions like a mouse click. A very good answer would also provide an example script that handled something like a mouseover event.

   The answer should explain how multimedia elements can improve the Web page by making it more engaging, and adding more layers of communication as noted in Chapter 1. You should be able to write down how multimedia is added to a Web page.

   A good answer would also explain how applications built with multimedia authoring tools like Director which included interactivity, animation and multimedia can also be added to Web pages.

2. This question is similar to the previous one, however the emphasis is on the issues and problems rather than how advanced features are added. You should explain what CSS and DHTML are and also how multimedia can be added to a Web page. For each of these aspects you can then explain what the issues are. For CSS and DHTML the issues are the incompatibility of browsers, particularly between Netscape and Microsoft, and the inability of earlier generation browsers to understand CSS and DHTML.

   There are a number of issues involved in the inclusion of multimedia in a Web page. The first issue you should mention is the variety of plug-in players that are installed on user computers and therefore the lack of control of how your Web pages might appear. The second issue is the size of media files and the need to try to 'nibble' them down using techniques like resampling. The other solution to deal with large media files is to stream them but this again involves the problem of ensuring users have the right plug-in installed.

3. This question is asking you to explain what each of the components of DHTML-scripting, CSS and the document object model are. You could start by explaining how each element works and then show with the aid of an example like a rollover how the three elements interact to create a dynamic effect.

4. You should start your answer by discussing the phenomenon of technology convergence and how computers, televisions, personal data assistants and tele-communications are all beginning to offer services usually offered via the others. You can then give some examples from each of these technologies – viewing video files on 3G mobile phones.

Section 6

Further reading

Reading

http://www.w3schools.com this site contains many useful tutorials on HTML and other Web development techniques.

Goodman, D. (2002) *Dynamic HTML: The Definitive Reference, 2nd Edition, A Comprehensive Resource for HTML, CSS, DOM & JavaScript,* O'Reilly & Associates, Inc.

Flanagan, D. (2001) *JavaScript: The Definitive Guide, 4th Edition,* O'Reilly & Associates, Inc.

Index